BLACK CHILDREN'S PERCEPTION OF THE USE OF THEIR DIALECT

LUBERTA F. MAYS

San Francisco, California
1977

Published By

R & E RESEARCH ASSOCIATES, INC.
4843 Mission Street, San Francisco 94112

Publishers

Robert D. Reed and Adam S. Eterovich

Library of Congress Card Catalog Number

77-081030

I.S.B.N.

0-88247-481-2

ACKNOWLEDGMENTS

I wish to express my deep appreciation and lasting gratitude to Professors Ann Marie Mueser and Patrick C. Lee whose guidance and understanding gave me the confidence to bring this study to fruition. It could not have been done without their expert guidance and insightfulness.

Respect and love to my husband, Frederick, and to my sons Jeffrey, Fredrick, Robert, Gregory and Michael for their steadfast support and belief that, "Mommie, you can do it!"

TABLE OF CONTENTS

Chapter   Page

      ACKNOWLEDGMENTS iii

I   INTRODUCTION 1

      Background of the Study 2

        Parents, School and Reading Programs 2

        Dialect Speakers in School 3

        Sight Basal Reader 5

        Linguistic Approach 6

        Auditory Discrimination and
          Reading Achievement 8

        Auditory Perception and Black Dialect 9

        Perception of Dialect Speech by Teachers 9

      Need for the Present Study 12

      Operational Definitions 13

      Statement of Problem and Hypotheses 14

II   REVIEW OF LITERATURE 16

      Phonology and Graphology 17

      Phonology and Orthography 24

      Conclusion 28

      Limitations of Previous Studies 29

III METHODS 31

      Selection of Neighborhood 31

      Selection of School 32

Chapter   Page

              Selection of Subjects   33

              Racial Background and Speech Patterns of
                 Teachers and Researcher   34

              Selection of Words   35

              Design of Study   36

     IV   RESULTS AND CONCLUSIONS   46

     V   DISCUSSION AND SOME IMPLICATIONS   61

              Discussion in Dialect Speech and
                 Perception of Dialect   63

              Discussion of Dialect Speech and
                 Orthography   74

              Recommendations for Teachers of Black
                 Dialect Speaking Children   79

              Limitations of Present Study   80

              Recommendations for Further Research   81

BIBLIOGRAPHY   84

APPENDIX A   89

APPENDIX B   90

APPENDIX C   97

LIST OF TABLES

Table	Page
1 Four Schools in District 28 Queens	32
2 School, Class, Sex, Age, Reading Approach and Teacher's Race	34
3 List From Which Words Were Chosen for Part One, Two and Three and Phonological Characteristic Studied	37
4 Percent of Students in Each Class With Specified Dialect Speech Characteristics	53
5 Total Number and Percent of Children in Three Classes With Specified Dialect Speech Characteristics	55
6 Results of Correlation for Individual Classes and Overall for Hypothesis I	56
7 Results of Correlation for Individual Classes and Overall for Hypothesis II	57
8 Analysis of Variance Among Reading Groups	59

LIST OF FIGURES

Figure   Page

1   Incidences of Dialect Speech for Class I (Verbal) 48

2   Incidence of Dialect Speech for Class II (Verbal) 48

3   Incidences of Dialect Speech for Class III (Verbal) 48

4   Incidences of Dialect Speech for Class I (Auditory) 49

5   Incidences of Dialect Speech for Class II (Auditory) 49

6   Incidences of Dialect Speech for Class III (Auditory) 49

7   Incidences of Dialect Speech for Class I (Visual) 50

8   Incidences of Dialect Speech for Class II (Visual) 50

9   Incidences of Dialect Speech for Class III (Visual) 50

10   Mean Dialect Speech on Part I, II, and III for Individual Classes 52

CHAPTER I

INTRODUCTION

Language patterns of young Black school children have been an increasingly important focus of teachers, linguists and school administrators for the past few years. The relationship of language patterns to reading achievement is a significant aspect of this focus. Researchers have examined the relationship of various components of reading programs to language patterns of Black dialect speakers in search of answers to reading problems. The present study posits that knowledge of phonemes used by many Black second graders in New York City public schools, and knowledge of how the child perceives the language he uses in terms of "right" or "wrong" might be a missing link for teachers in planning an effective reading program for these children. It was the purpose of this study to find the relationship between the incidence of Black English and the child's perception that Black English is not preferred speech. The study examined the Black child's verbal quality of speech, his preference for dialect or standard speech when heard together, and his ability to identify visually the standard spelling of a word when that word is paired with its counterpart in dialect spelling. The study also looked at the relationship between dialect speech and the reading approach used to teach a group of children. This four part study first, established language styles of Black second graders through recording phonemic characteristics of their speech; second, asked the youngster to judge "rightness" of words pronounced both in dialect and standard English; third, examined the relationship between use of dialect speech and the ability to identify words written in traditional orthography; and finally, contrasted groups using dialect speech where different approaches of teaching reading were used.

Background of the Study

Parents are concerned about reading success and approaches teachers use in attempting to teach children to read.

Parents, School and Reading Programs

Many parents see successful reading as the vehicle which will move their children into the mainstream of society. Schools are interested in reading success because they feel it is the key to the communications process and will unlock a variety of experiences which would otherwise remain unexplored. Listening, speaking, reading, and the ability to understand are all vital parts of one's language experience. Not only is the knowledge of how these three components relate to each other important, but of similar importance is the relationship of these components to the language styles and culture of the youngster being taught.

Black children's speech is of interest to some linguists, because of their interest in comparing development and use of dialect speech with development and use of standard English speech sounds. Labov (1967a), Baratz (1969), and Stewart (1969) have made studies of the relationship of Black children's speech and their success in reading. These linguists have observed that speech used by the Black child outside of school is quite different from speech patterns the child is expected to master and use in school. Concurrent to this, dialects used outside of school are neither understood or accepted by teachers in the school setting. Both Labov (1967a) and Stewart (1969) discuss the effect of this on reading success in school.

Baratz (1969), Stewart (1971), and Leaverton (1968) all see the reading process as being delayed and hindered because of the difference in language styles between Black urban children and white standard English speaking children. Baratz (1969), and Stewart (1969) recommend first teaching the child to read in his mother tongue. In this case the mother tongue is Black English.

Leaverton and Gladney (1968), feel there should be a simultaneous approach which handles Black English and standard English in the same text. Leaverton and Gladney (1968) proposed and instituted such a program which was studied in Chicago. The results indicated no statistically significant differences in use of verb forms between the experimental and control groups. However, there was a trend toward use of standard English verb form in the experimental group.

Linguists and educators have shown continued interest in finding the relationship between some Black children's language and their poor reading achievement. Low reading scores in predominantly Black school districts are of utmost importance, and yet, a puzzle to educators.

Dialect Speakers in School

Each linguist has his own terminology for expressing language variations of Blacks. Labov (1967a) calls the speech of some Black urban children "Non-Standard English." Dillard (1972) uses the term "Black English." Bailey (1969) prefers to use the term "Black Dialect," while Stewart (1969) uses

"Negro Non-Standard English." These terms are all synonomous and represent some divergence from the speech of white standard speaking children.

Children who speak Black dialect may have tremendous problems of speech identity when placed in an unfamiliar cultural environment. For some Black children, school culture and home culture are similar, but for many others, school is considered another cultural experience. When one considers the life style and language of some urban Black children, it is not difficult to understand that the school culture would be foreign to these children, and could conceivably result in some cultural conflict.

Baratz and Shuy (1969) suggest that the failure of large numbers of Black children to perform at, or above national norms on reading achievement tests may be due, at least in part, to the fact that these children do not speak standard English, the language of instruction and the language of the text, when they come to school. When coming to school, Black children who use dialect speech have to cope with two styles of speech: the dialect speech which they and their families use and the standard speech used by their teachers. Baratz (1969) states:

> Because the educational system has been ineffective in coping with teaching inner-city children to read, it treats reading failure (in terms of grading and ranking, etc.) as if this failure were due to intellectual deficits of the child rather than to methodological inadequacies in teaching procedures. Thus the system is unable to teach the child to read, but very quickly teaches him to regard himself as intellectually inadequate, and therefore of low self worth and low social value (p. 11).

Moreover, standard English is so inbred in New York City school teachers, that a teacher may become hostile to Black children's dialect. When a school is overtly hostile to the child's dialect, the child has real questions about the value of his language.

4

Educators have tried a variety of approaches in attempting to teach children to become involved in the reading process. Three familiar types of approaches used in New York City public schools are as follows:

1. Phonetic approach
2. Sight Basal Reader approach
3. Linguistic approach

Proponents of the phonetic approach feel that a phonics trained child has no trouble recognizing words previously learned, that he can use pronunciation as a key to unlocking the sound of new words, that the child is more likely to pronounce words "correctly" and can therefore read well and with ease. They also feel that comprehension follows naturally (New York City Board of Education, 1967).

Sight Basal Reader

This approach does not emphasize phonics as a way of teaching reading to children. Those who oppose phonics as a way of teaching reading, refer to the "unphonetic" spelling of English, with its multiplicity of ways to indicate single vowel and consonant sounds. They claim that the detailed word analysis sacrifices interest in reading and slows down thought. Therefore, they claim, comprehension is lost. These are the characteristics of the Sight Basal Reader approach:

1. The teaching technique takes the children from the general (whole words) to the specific (word parts [opposite of phonics approach]).

2. Word recognition developed through patterns, special features of word (e.g., double letter), recognition of known parts of words, contextual clues, picture clues, phonetic clues, structural analysis, or a

combination of these approaches (New York City Board of Education, 1967).

Linguistic Approach

This method of teaching reading is claimed to be the newest of the three approaches discussed in the present study. The linguistic approach disregards meaning completely in its beginning stages. The entire emphasis is on sound, and nonsense syllables are suggested at times to supplement the practice of recognizing one-syllable words. The characteristics of the program are as follows:

1. Combines resources of eye and ear as basic elements of learning.

2. Enlargement of the power to identify words from patterns of letters.

3. Translation of letters into sounds, and sounds into meaning becomes increasingly automatic.

4. Cumulatively builds up the child's independence and confidence (New York City Board of Education).

The program follows the following steps:

1. Learning alphabet capitals and small letters.

2. Left to right movement across page.

3. Progress from top to bottom of page.

4. One syllable words carefully grouped according to sounds (e.g., can, fan, pan, etc.).

Certain characteristics of the linguistic and phonetic approach are very much alike. They both emphasize use of patterns and structural analysis for purposes of word recognition. They both also utilize phonetic clues for word recognition purposes. One of the main differences is that the phonetic approach emphasizes the technique of "sounding out" words, which is then followed by reading the letters and parts of words, based on sound.

Although the "Sight Basal Reader" approach does not emphasize phonetics, there is a component to this program which deals directly and precisely with phonics as a technique in analyzing words. Most Black children in New York City schools are exposed to the phonetic approach, in varying degrees, as the process by which they're expected to learn to decode. Although the three approaches discussed have stated their expected outcomes clearly and succinctly, many Black urban school children have fallen short of these expectations.

The New York Times (November 19, 1972) recently reported that the reading problem defies any simple solutions, as reading ability of pupils in New York elementary schools continue to decline. The report stated that of the system's 632 elementary schools, only 163 had at least half their pupils reading at or above the norm for their grade. As stated:

> An analysis of the new report shows, as expected, that the schools with the highest proportion of youngsters reading at or above grade are generally those in white middle-class neighborhoods, such as the Whitestone area of Queens and the Riverdale section of the Bronx and that those with the lowest proportions are in poor neighborhoods (p. 76).

The annual report on reading for 1973 indicated that reading scores were beginning to show an incline. Schools in Black and poor neighborhoods, however, remained at the lowest level (New York Times, February 14, 1974).

Auditory Discrimination and
   ## Reading Achievement

C. Deutsch (1964) feels that the ability to read is directly related to auditory discrimination. Her study indicated that poor readers at
grade one, three, and five had poor auditory discrimination. Auditory discrimination is the ability to recognize differences and similarities in
sounds. Durrell (1953) defines it as the "ability to identify sounds in the
spoken word."

Researchers have found a significant relationship between auditory
discrimination and reading ability and achievement. Thompson (1963) compared
auditory discrimination scores of first grade children with later reading
achievement scores. In her longitudinal study, all children entering first
grade in a mid-western town were tested in auditory discrimination and at the
end of second grade were given reading achievement tests.→She found auditory
discrimination ability to be highly correlated with success in primary reading and concluded that the first graders' auditory discrimination ability is
indeed a predictor of who will become a good reader. The questions to be
asked are: Should ability to identify sounds in spoken words be limited to
standard English sounds? Or, if one's usage contains non-standard sounds,
does that prevent the identification of standard sounds? "Sounding out"
words has been considered a key process in breaking the code for first grade
readers for many years. If a child displayed an inability to do this, he
was not considered ready to begin a reading program. The "sounds," of course,
were always based on standard English phonology. It seems quite evident,
therefore, that readiness to read is not based on the child's ability to
discriminate sounds in the spoken word, but instead, on the ability to discriminate between the standard English sounds in the spoken word. It is,

therefore, conceivable that children who speak non-standard English are not reading because the teachers feel they are not ready to begin. The present study, which asks the child to judge which one of the two spoken sounds is "right," is indicative of his ability to identify the sounds in both standard and non-standard English.

Auditory Perception and
Black Dialect

Labov, Cohen and Robbins (1965) tested the auditory perception of his Black subjects as a possible approach to the reading problem. He specifically wanted to know if his subjects were aware of words ending in the -ed suffix. The results were that the subjects could not detect the absence of -ed. Instead, they corrected the verb usage in the sentence. However, the children were not asked to make a value judgment about the way they perceived their language. Similarly, in a Chicago study conducted by Leaverton and Gladney (1968), it was emphasized strongly that, while attempting to examine the child's ability to discriminate between sounds, they chose not to have the child focus on making a value judgment about the language style he used.

Perception of Dialect Speech
by Teachers

A large piece of the present study focuses specifically on the child's perception of his dialect speech. This aspect of the Black child's language desperately needs to be examined from the teacher's point of view as well. There is a small body of research which indicates that dialects used by Black children are perceived negatively by white teachers, and mark the user as inferior to members of other groups (Putnam and O'Hern, 1955).

Woodworth (1971) stated that teachers were inclined to judge the character
and worth of an individual from his manner of speaking. These impressions
sometimes carry over into the teacher's evaluation of a child's school performance.

Woodworth and Salzer (1971) did a study designed to furnish
evidence as to the validity of such an expectation. Drawn from five graduate
education classes at a college in Western New York, a total of 119 elementary
teachers were the subjects of the investigation. During two 45 minute ses-
sions, separated by an interval of three weeks, these teachers listened to
and evaluated what were presented as children's recorded social studies
reports. Identical reports were read by Black and white sixth grade male
students; that is, at the second session the Black student presented the
same material which the white child had read at the first meeting, and vice
versa. Recorded instructions were played for the subjects at the beginning
of each session. No mention of race was made or any purposes of the investigator discussed. Examination of the data revealed a consistent statistical
difference between teacher's evaluations of materials presented orally by
Black and white children. For each of the variables, white students received
a substantially higher rating than the Black students for identical material.
The researcher made it quite clear that the Black children read the material
as written in standard English and did not alter syntax or substitute Black
lexical variants. Neither did they deviate substantially from the conven-
tional pronunciation of words. Teachers involved apparently picked up
paralinguistic clues (e.g., intonation pattern) to identify the race of the
child. With that identification made, the subjects downgraded what was
felt to be the Black child's report, thus providing evidence of teacher
bias against Black students.

Another study which examined the reading responses of Black children, and the possibility of being incorrectly evaluated by white teachers was "Black Reading Errors or White Teacher Biases?" conducted by Rystrom and Cowart (1972). These researchers suggested that teachers are hired to teach children to use language effectively and to read well. It is said that they have the right to modify children's behavior in order to achieve these goals. Rystrom and Cowart feel, however, that too little attention has been paid to the concomitant obligation of learning to understand the dialect. The question to be answered was: does this dialect interference have educational consequences? That is, are the reading responses of Black children often incorrectly evaluated. Two teachers, one Black and one white, were selected for the experiment. Each teacher administered section one and two of the Dolch Basic Sight Word Test (1942) to second graders. There were an equal number of Black and white students in each group. It was found that the race of the tester had a significant effect upon the decoding scores of the subjects. Black students evaluated by the white teacher read fewer words correctly than the students in the other three combinations of teacher and pupil race.

These findings were supported by Fleming (1970), who found that linguistically unsophisticated reading teachers responded to dialectal deviations as if they were reading errors. He concluded that many teachers confuse norms of speaking with reading performance variables. This is more likely to happen where the teacher's speech differs considerably from that of the children.

Rystrom and Cowart (1972) argue that it is important for teachers to "tune in" on Black speech. The first proposed step is to recognize

Black speech as a valuable dialect with its own set of patterned features. The second step they suggest is to learn which of these features occur in the student's speech, but not in the teacher's speech. Finally, they predict that, in the process of learning to hear their students, teachers would learn to discriminate between reading errors and dialect variations. They would then no longer discriminate against children whose dialect speech is different.

Baratz (1971) indicated strong feelings about teacher attitude and Black dialect speech. She stated:

> Most of (the Black child's) middle class teachers have wrongly viewed his language as pathological, disordered, "lazy speech." This failure to recognize the interference from the child's different linguistic system and consequent negative teacher attitudes toward the child and his language lead directly to reading difficulties and subsequent school failure (p. 12).

Need for the Present Study

Although New York City Black school children have been exposed to a variety of approaches, there is still widespread failure in teaching them to read (New York Times, October 23, 1973). Educators are still questioning the reason for failure in low socioeconomic areas. What occurs when children do not meet teacher expectations in terms of learning standard pronunciations? That question becomes compounded with the possibility that there is some confusion in the minds of teachers, in regard to the child's process of encoding and decoding. That is, teachers do not really know the mental processes children use in transforming messages into code, or converting that code into plain text. Educators must attempt to find answers to questions, not previously asked about the language of Black children, if they are to become more effective in teaching them how to read. What seems to be needed first, is finding out what speech variations the child uses, and next, how he perceives his language. Since Labov (1967a) and Leaverton and Gladney (1968) did not wish to become involved with the value judgment component of the speech of dialect speaking children, the present study attempted to gain some insight into the stated preferences of Black children for language they speak and hear. Educators also need to know specifically whether use of dialect prevents identification of words written in standard orthography. Since there is currently insufficient research addressed to the questions raised, the need for additional research is apparent.

The present researcher envisioned information gained from such a study as vitally important, if more effective reading programs are to be initiated in the public schools. The results of this study, coupled with results of previous research about Black children and their language, should provide some insight into the reading problems of some Black school children. Given the size of the problem, no avenue should go unexplored in the search for answers about reading failure.

Operational Definitions

Dialect: According to Dillard (1972):

> Dialect, as used in linguistics, has none of the opprobrium attached to the term in such popular phrases as dialect comedy, etc. It is a collection of idialects; that is, the speech pattern of a number of individuals whose language is similar in some significant way (p. 300).

Orthography: Correct or standard spelling.

Phonology: According to Dillard (1972):

> Phonology is the systematic study of
> the sound patterns of language--either
> language in general terms of "Universal"
> phonology or by an individual language
> (p. 302).

He indicates that the layman uses the term "pronunciation" for what linguists mean by phonology.

Standard English: According to Dillard (1972):

> A standard language (or dialect) is
> one which has achieved official recognition
> in terms of having written grammatical
> descriptions (especially if they prescribe
> "correct" usage), distionaries and printed
> works with complete expositions (not just
> passages of dialogue) in the language
> (p. 303).

Statement of Problem and Hypotheses

Many Black school children, who use dialect speech, are not reading as well as their white counterparts in school. Teachers and parents know that the primary focus of schooling is on reading. The problem which faces parents, teachers, and linguists about Black dialect speech and reading success is threefold. First, perhaps due to differences in background, culture, and education, there is a misconception about phonological variations in Black dialect speech. Second, there may be some conflict between the teacher's and the child's perception of dialect speech. Third, there is an assumption that dialect speech interferes with the child's ability to attain reading skills.

The present study examined the following hypotheses:

1. There is a positive correlation between the incidence of dialect speech of Black second graders and their perception that dialect speech is "bad."

2. Use of dialect speech does not interfere with the dialect speaker's ability to identify words in traditional orthography.

CHAPTER II

REVIEW OF LITERATURE

In his study of "The non-standard vernacular of the Negro community" Labov (1967a) notes:

> ...despite wide-spread resistance to the notion, that there is a similarity in the speech of Negro children in northern urban centers, due not to any racial genetic, or physiological feature (but to) a culturally inherited pattern...transmitted to the centers of most northern cities by migrants from the South (p. 2).

Various aspects of this dialect are discussed based on data from the author's own research. Labov argues that there are a different set of speech rules governing Negro non-standard vernacular. When speech rules are different he says "A child has no clues to the standard spelling differences from his own speech patterns...and may have difficulty recognizing many words in their standard spelling (p. 145)." He indicates that Negro dialect differs from standard English both in grammar and phonology. From the standpoint of learning to read, some of these differences present handicaps, especially those in which phonological differences coincide with grammatical differences. This sometimes results in the existence of a large number of homonyms in the speech of Negro children different from those of the teacher. Some of these phonological variables are: (1) "r-lessness" which produces homonyms such as guard-god, sore=saw, etc.; (2) "l-lessness" which results in toll=toe, tool=too, and fault=fought, etc.; (3) simplification of consonant clusters so that past=pass, wind=win, rift=riff, mend=men and hold=hole, etc.

Dillard (1972) is of the same opinion. In addition to words pronounced as homonyms, other words pronounced by some Black children have a different pronunciation from standard English. For example, help sound like hep, four sounds like foh, and car sounds like caa. Bailey, in her 1968 study notes that in Black dialect speech there is a substitution for the sound "th" in initial, medial, and final positions. Because of these substitutions, that sounds like dat, mouth like mouf, and breath like breve. She also suggests that speakers of Black dialect lose final unstressed syllables or simplify consonant clusters by adding "es" in place of final "s" to make a word plural. For example, tests become tesses, desks becomes desses, and ghosts becomes ghosses. Labov (1967) and Bailey (1968) agree that other phonological variables which cause lack of distinction between words are evidenced in pin - pen, beer - bear, poor - pour and picture - pitcher.

Singh and Black (1966) in related research, recorded English, Hindu and Japanese native speakers pronouncing 26 consonants, some not phonemic in the speaker's own language. The purpose of the study was to establish speaker-listener relationship in the perception of these consonants (a) when both belonged to the same language groups, and (b) when both were of different groups. The results were that speakers and listeners were most able when producing and perceiving sounds of their native tongue.

Phonology and Graphology

Melmed (1970) investigated the relationship between Black English phonology and the reading process. In his study he constructed tests of auditory discrimination, oral and silent reading comprehension and speech production involving the five phonological differences which Labov (1967b) cited as possible sources of interference between the phonologies of standard English and Negro non-standard English. Melmed found that Black subjects did significantly more poorly than white and other subjects (primarily Mexican Americans) on the auditory discrimination and oral production tests, but did not differ from disadvantaged whites and Mexican Americans in reading competence in standard English. Melmed's study emphasized clearly that the poor auditory discrimination did not play a significant role in the child's reading progress. Nor did the child's dialect speech, using phonological variations cited by Labov, prevent him from reading as well as children from different ethnic groups. Thus, the onus was placed on the social class rather than on the dialect speech of a particular ethnic group.

C. Deutsch (1964) investigated auditory discrimination as a factor in verbal behavior and in reading achievement of a lower class group. She postulated that children raised in a very noisy environment with little directed and sustained speech stimulation might well be deficient in their discrimination and recognition of speech sounds. She felt that these children would have difficulty with any other skills which are primarily dependent on good auditory discrimination. One could consider that reading is such a skill.

In Labov's study (1967b) he tested the auditory perception of Black subjects, as a possible approach to the study of language differences. Perception in this sense dealt only with the youngster's ability to hear differences in speech sounds and not the child's evaluation of his language. The purpose of the test was to look at the use of the _ed_ suffix in Black dialect speech. Subjects were asked to change certain sentences to correct classroom

18

English. The result was that youngsters had little ability to detect the absence of _ed_ as a grammatical element to be corrected. Instead, they proceeded to correct the verb usage which they did perceive as incorrect. Although the Labov study did not ask the child to place a value judgment on any choice of words, the classroom correction test did ask the child to change a stated sentence to "correct classroom English." In so doing the implication was made that any other way of stating that sentence would be incorrect. Presenting the question in such a way, perhaps provided information to the subject about the researcher's perception of his dialect speech.

In a program, designed out of Leaverton and Gladney's study (1968) called "The Reading Series," Leaverton, et al, introduced the concept of "Everyday Talk" and "School Talk." Everyday talk refers to the non-standard pattern of English with respect to verb usage. Perception was stressed only in terms of the child's ability to hear the difference between "School Talk" and "Everyday Talk." Leaverton emphasized strongly that no value as right or wrong, correct or incorrect were used in this model. They stressed that teachers in Chicago considered non-standard dialect a serious problem and that children were corrected constantly. In order to encourage communications between teachers of standard English and non-standard speaking children, they suggested that the learning sequence in teaching standard speech patterns should start with an actual statement made by the child. It would then be possible to make a transition from the child's dialect to standard English by adding to the child's dialect. This study focused on the grammar of the dialect speaker and not the phonology of his language. Conversations of Afro-American children from four low income ghetto areas were taped. The tapes were analyzed and four differences in verb usage were identified as focal points of the proposed program. First, the verbs _is_ and _are_ were omitted.

19

Second, one verb form was used for all subjects in the past tense, and fourth, "Be" was used in place of is, am and are in certain kinds of sentences. These differences were used as the basis of the training program.

Instructional sequences began with rhymed pattern practices, then materials were designed to help the child make the transition at a conscious level from Black to standard dialect. The procedure which was followed was that the teacher told the children a story or asked a question which elicited from the children the speech pattern in the verb area studied. Although the children's statements were non-standard, the teacher recorded them in standard form on the blackboard. For example, in a sentence like "Gregory brown just like me," she recorded, Gregory is brown, just like me. The teacher described the sentence in "Everyday Talk" and "School Talk," explaining to the children that sentences that omit is, are "Everyday Talk" and sentences that include is are "School Talk" (p. 760). Leaverton and Gladney make it clear that "Everyday Talk" and "School Talk" are different ways of expressing ideas. She further indicates that neither one is "wrong" or "right" but are sentences used in different situations, in school and out of school. Verb usage in "School Talk" was reinforced through sentences given to the children, where they were expected to change non-standard dialect to standard dialect in oral sentences. Experimental and matched control groups were used. These groups were examined separately, and no significant differences were found between the groups with respect to two forms of verbs, i.e., the conditional with Be form, and the regular present (inclusion of "s" to verbs). With other verb forms, the findings indicated the experimental group used more standard English than the control group, but the trends were not statistically significant. An important factor cited by the researcher was that the model encouraged the teacher to

20

respect and accept the children's established dialect and at the same time provide a framework to help children recognize, learn, and hopefully begin to use standard English.

The present study focused directly on the dialect speaking child's perception of his dialect speech. Hopefully, when the teacher is aware of how the child perceives his dialect, positive relations about the child's language may begin to develop, and teachers and students will not be operating at cross purposes.

Stewart (1971), a proponent of dialect readers, feels that "Negro children are burdened with achievement barriers in the form of extra (and uncompensated for) language-learning requirements (p. 368)." He explains that all children are expected to learn to read in school but for Negro children the problem is more difficult because of their inability to see the sound-spelling relationship and grammatical patterns with which standard English speaking children are quite familiar.

Similarly, Baratz (1971) indicated that when the middle class child begins the process of learning to read, his problem is primarily one of decoding the graphic representation of a language with which he is already familiar. She feels that the Black child's problem is doubled since he not only has to learn to decode words, but he must also translate them into his own language. Thus, she stated:

> This presents him with an almost insurmountable obstacle since the written words frequently do not go together in any pattern that is familiar or meaningful to him. He is baffled by this confrontation with (1) a necessity to learn the meaning of graphic symbols, and (2) a new language with its new syntax; (3) a vague (or not so vague depending upon the cultural and linguistic sophistication of the teacher) sense that there is something wrong with his language (p. 20).

Baratz (1970a) conducted a study with 481 Black first and second graders in Washington, D. C. parochial schools. In the study, disadvantaged Black and lower middle class white children were administered a repetition task involving standard and non-standard English sentences. Results indicated that Black children performed significantly better than white children on the non-standard stimuli. The converse was true for the standard sentences. She explained that the results of this research clearly indicated that there are two dialects involved in the educational complex of Black children; that Black children are generally not bidialectal; that there is evidence of interference from their dialect when Black children attempt to use standard English; and that language assessment of disadvantaged Blacks must involve measures of their knowledge of non-standard English as well as additional measures of their knowledge of standard English. She suggests there is difficulty in code switching when the second code is not as well learned as the first.

Bailey (1967) indicated that Black children operate under many of the handicaps of non-English speaking children. She said the resemblance of their language gives them no advantage in acquiring effective use of English or in understanding all that is taught in this mode. She further indicates that well-known features in the language of Black children represent parts of an identifiable structure which differs from English in grammar and sound system. Bailey concludes that the most serious difficulties arise not in vocabulary but in structurally based phonological differences which result in a set of homonyms unfamiliar to teachers and not found in textbooks. Her proposal is to teach dialect speaking children to speak standard English prior to teaching them to read. In this way she feels there will be no linguistic conflict caused by exposing the child to standard English in beginning readers.

Goodman (1969) feels that the child is well on the way to mastering his own language by the time he is five years of age. He feels that teachers underestimate the competencies that the child brings to school with him. Children have much more strength to build on than weaknesses to overcome. One needs only to listen and realize that children from lower socio-economic groups have mastered the language of their communities and can communicate their thoughts and ideas to people most important to them in language which their listeners easily understand. Goodman, a proponent of standardized spelling indicates that, no matter how words are pronounced, printers across the country usually spell them the same way. What is relevant to the teacher is the presence or absence of distinction between two words that sound alike. He emphasized that it really makes little difference how the child pronounces the word <u>pen</u>, what counts is whether or not this word is distinct from <u>pin</u> for the child. Johnson and Simons (1972) stress that children should be allowed to impose their own phonological systems on standard English spellings. In their writings they discuss the necessity of having a complete understanding of language variation spoken by the child, including understanding of its phonology and grammar. After teachers have this understanding of Black children, their culture and language, they must adapt their teaching strategies accordingly. They feel it is important for teachers to understand the nature of the conflict that arises when the child's language is rejected, either explicitly or implicitly by the teachers. They emphasize that teachers must be aware of conflict points between Black dialect and standard English. This knowledge will enable them to make the important distinction between reading errors which must be corrected and pronunciation differences which are dialectal and can, therefore, be safely ignored. Regarding the phonetic approach to teaching of reading, they stress that teachers should be aware that blending phonics methods may create problems because they exaggerate conflict points and thus might confuse the children being taught. Educators continue to ask questions regarding the phoneme-grapheme relationship, especially as it relates to dialect speaking children. Linguists and orthographers are continuing to research these areas in an effort to secure some answers for themselves and teachers.

Concerning this problem, Stewart (1969) suggests:

> If the differences (between SE and NNE phonology) are regular enough, which they often are, then the Negro dialect speaker may be able to set up his own sound-spelling correspondence between them...ones which will be different from those set up by a speaker of SE, but which will allow effective word identification nevertheless (p. 3).

He advocates the design of a phonics program that makes the sound-spelling correspondence between SE orthography and NNE phonology explicit for the child.

Phonology and Orthography

Smith (1972) has done extensive writing on phonology, orthography, reading, and writing. He feels that sounds of words represent a compromise between speakers and listeners. Speakers prefer minimal difference within phonemic clusters and listeners prefer maximum differences. He maintains that slurred speech is easier to produce than speech in which every difference is clearly articulated, but not so easy to understand. Listening, on the other hand, would be easier if there were no word pairs distinguished by a single feature only, such as "bet" and "pet," or "bet" and "bed."

In reference to visual identification of words based on the sounds of letters, he feels the visual system is so constrained in the amount of information that it can process that we have no time to identify every word, let alone every letter. Decoding into sound is quite unnecessary for comprehending written language. The fact that there is unexpected spelling of some words indicate that we do not normally understand written words on the basis of their sounds but instead attend directly to the meaning of the particular spelling. Smith further indicates that the relationship of phonics to the manner in which even beginning readers actually identify words new in their experience is largely imaginary. He maintains that the phonics approach is easy--provided one knows how a word is pronounced in the first place. In relation to the reader and word identification, Smith feels there are distinct strategies which the reader uses for identifying words. First, he says readers look at words and recognize them through visual configuration. He calls this direct or immediate word identification: not immediate in terms of instantaneous occurrence, but in the sense that it is not mediated by the identification of sub units, such as individual letters, or spelling units, or syllables. He says that the fact that the spelling has some relationship to the sound of the word is irrelevant to the recognition process because spelling itself is not examined during the reading act.

Other strategies that we have for word identification problems are acquired quite unconsciously and are subject to our awareness. Meaning is deduced non-alphabetically and we go from meaning to sound rather than construct the sound in order to get the meaning. Smith firmly believes that the connection between written language and speech matters less than is often assumed, especially that between phonology and orthography. The sound-spelling relationship has practically nothing to do with immediate reading. The relationship between orthography and phonology may be used as a last and partial strategy for word identification. However, he feels the strategies mentioned above seem far more likely to be analogic devices based on knowledge that we have acquired unconsciously, just as we have unconsciously acquired our knowledge or how to distinguish dogs from cats. Finally, Smith (1972) feels that the mere fact that sound-spelling correspondences exist does not necessarily entail that they are of critical importance in reading.

In a study by Kligman, Cronnell, and Verna (1972) the phonology of Black English as it relates to spelling was examined. These researchers maintained that dialect interference in spelling has been largely ignored. They felt that, because spelling is based on oral stimuli, it is quite possible that there is greater potential for dialect interferences in spelling than in reading. It was their belief that dialect pronunciation may interfere with the spelling of unfamiliar words for Black English speakers in the same way that standard pronunciation may interfere with the spelling of unfamiliar irregularly spelled words for standard English speakers. For example, Black English speakers who do not pronounce the (1) in "wild" might mistakenly spell it as "wide," just as a standard English speaker might mistakenly spell "half" as "haff."

Kligman, et al, devised spelling tests to be administered to second grade children. Test items were written including three examples of each of 43 pronunciation features derived from the description of Black English phonology. A multiple choice spelling test was administered. For each word, one or two errors were constructed which would reflect a likely Black English pronunciation. For example, since it was expected that a Black English speaking child might pronounce the word "mouth" as /mouf/ or /mout/, the errors constructed for "mouth" were "mouf" and "mout." The results of the study supported at least one of their hypotheses that dialect pronunciation has a significant relationship to the number and type of spelling errors made. These researchers do note however, that while Black English speakers clearly made more dialect related errors, white children had some of the same dialect-related spelling difficulties that Black children had. Although pronunciation differences in Black English were significantly related to the spelling output of those children who speak dialect, only selected features caused enough difficulty to cause concern. These researchers feel that their study justifies special spelling instruction for Black English speakers.

Venezky (1970) states that a linguist can provide reliable data on the pronunciation of a language, the feature of its writing system, and the relationship between speech and writing but he cannot, as a linguist, decide how such revelations should be deployed in the teaching of spelling. The reasons for this are that the linguist's descriptions are inferences, that is, while he is describing language habits, he cannot observe them directly but must infer them from observations of behavior. Next, effectiveness for teaching spelling depends not just upon the linguistic nature of the spelling materials, but also upon the learning ability, teaching ability, and school setting.

In reference to spelling programs and dialect speakers Venezky indicates that a rational spelling program, regardless of its pedagogy, must be based upon the speech which the learner uses and not upon an idealized dialect (standard English), replete with synthetic syllable breaks and un-reduced vowels. He further notes that spelling is not reading and says wholly new patterns must be derived starting with sound and working toward spelling. This cannot be achieved through a simple reversal of spelling to sound patterns, but must come from careful analysis.

Thus, he indicated clearly that there is a need for a more rational spelling program. This theory is supported by Stewart (1969) and Labov (1967a). These writers all feel that spelling should be more related to the way one speaks. Venezky, however, stated emphatically that "spelling is not reading" and therefore there need be no interference in the dialect speakers ability to identify words in traditional orthography. Unlike many teachers of reading, Smith (1972) and Venezky (1970) feel that the sound-spelling relationship has little to do with immediate reading, and is perhaps one of the last strategies used in word identification by children.

Conclusion

Although research has proven to be beneficial for a large number of teachers, many others do not avail themselves of findings which might aid in program development. Some educators, even after extensive research has indicated otherwise, refuse to acknowledge the existence of Black dialect. Dillard (1972) maintains that the ignorant insistence by schools that Black English is either deviant or non-existent is ridiculous, since there can be no effective teaching and learning if the teacher is thoroughly locked into his own language mode and the students are locked into theirs. Baratz and Baratz (1970) cite that Black children have a well developed language system which should be "built on" if effective teaching is to become a reality for Black youngsters. They feel that the child's language should be the criterion on which language skills progress is based or there will be failure for the youngsters involved. They say that because the educational system has been ineffective in coping with teaching inner-city children to read, it treats reading failure as if it were due to intellectual deficits of the child rather than to methodological inadequacies in teaching procedure. Baratz (1971)

thinks the present system is unable to teach the child to read. In <u>Language</u>
<u>and Poverty</u> she says:

> The continued failure of programs of reading for
> ghetto children that offer more of the same, i.e.,
> more phonics, more word drills, etc., have indicated
> the need of a new orientation towards teaching inner
> city children to read. Any such program must take into
> account what is unique about the ghetto child that is
> impairing his ability to learn within the present system
> (p. 22).

In order to recognize that language patterns of some Black children
are different, not inferior, teachers should be thoroughly steeped in Black
culture. For a goodly number of the school population, the classroom provides
the setting for conflicts between the middle-class values that many teachers
espouse, and those of the lower socio-economic stratum of American society to
which some pupils are accustomed.

Limitations of Previous Studies

There are four major weaknesses of the studies previously discussed. First, little significant work has been done in the area of how the
youngster perceives the language he speaks. Second, major studies have
neglected to ask children to place a value judgment on their language. Third,
there is apparently no design where the child was asked to perform a word
recognition task when viewing dialect and standard orthography. Fourth, researchers have not identified differences in dialect speech of children on the
same grade level, using different reading approaches.

The present study addressed itself to these limitations in the
following ways. First, it obtained a wide range of dialect speech from each
subject. Then, it asked the child to listen to standard and non-standard

passages of speech. This determined whether the child could discriminate between sounds heard. Second, it asked the child to "be the judge" and to decide which spoken words he thought were "right." Third, the child saw a rendition of a dialect spelled word and a standard English word next to a picture and was asked to identify the word that went with the picture. Fourth, it compared dialect speech of children on the same grade level, but using different reading approaches. Hopefully, further information on these points will aid educators and linguists in solving some of the problems for school children who use Black dialect speech.

CHAPTER III

METHODS

The Black population in New York City supplies the largest ethnic group of children to the New York City Public School system. The New York Times (October 23, 1973) reports that the city's minority groups--the Blacks, the Hispanics and the Orientals--together account for the majority of students in two-thirds of the city's school districts.

Selection of Neighborhood

In examining the two largest ethnic categories one finds that Blacks total a school population of 406,974 (36.1%), while "others," the term used for whites of European heritage number 397,694 (35.2%). In the area of Queens where the present investigation was carried out, the enrollment totals 249,856. Blacks have an enrollment of 74,682 and European whites have an enrollment of 143,502. A further breakdown of the population of the school from which subjects were chosen for the present study gives a percentage of 99% Blacks, 1% Hispanics and 0% whites. Another school in the same district has a 97% Black student body. Two schools in the district which are predominantly white are P.S. #117 with only a 5.4% Black population, and P.S. #174 with a Black population of 9.8%. As the following table shows, there is a correspondence between the percentages of children reading at or above grade level and the racial population of the school.

Table 1

Four Schools in District 28 Queens

School	Black Population	Percent on or Above Grade Level
P.S. #40	99.0	33.2
P.S. #48	97.6	14.7
P.S. #117	5.4	65.5
P.D. #174	9.8	68.8

The percent of children reading on or above grade level is an accumulated percentage drawn from individual scores on the Metropolitan Achievement Test which is administered to all New York City Public School children.

Selection of School

The selection of the school was made on the basis of neighborhood, ethnic population, and speech patterns of the ethnic group. The public school was located in a low socio-economic section of Queens known as South Jamaica. The school is flanked by the "Jamaica Houses," a low income project. This project provides housing for many of the school children in the study. The neighborhood is 100 percent Black and therefore considered a ghetto area. The ethnic population is not the lone factor in determining this a ghetto area. A larger and more significant factor is that of poverty. This is significant because in urban cities "Black" and "poverty" are synonomous with "poor schooling." Moreover, poor schooling usually means low reading scores.

In order to determine phonology of children in the neighborhood and the school, the researcher and two teachers took a walking tour through the neighborhood and the school. Notations were made of their speech patterns at home and in school. Every child observed in the neighborhood had some of the speech characteristics cited in the work of Labov (1967a), Baratz (1969), Bailey (1968), and Dillard (1972). This was true to a lesser degree in the school setting. This indicated that perhaps children were attempting to control their regular speech patterns while in the school setting.

Selection of Subjects

Three groups of second grade boys and girls were used as subjects for the study. Ten boys and ten girls were randomly selected from each of three classroom groups of children, making a total of 60 children. The youngsters were between the ages of six and one half and eight years of age. The classes had been grouped heterogeneously, consisting of children with varying reading ability.

Two of the groups were reading from Basal readers; however, there was a very strong emphasis on use of phonics for teaching reading skills. Both of these groups not only used the same approach in learning to read, but they also used the same text for reading. The third group of children were being taught to read through a linguistic approach. As indicated by their reading scores on the Metropolitan Achievement Test, each child was well into the reading process at the time of the study. The tests for these subjects had been administered during the early Spring of 1973. The present study was conducted in the late Spring of the same school year.

Table 2

School, Class, Sex, Age, Reading Approach,

and Teacher's Race

School	Class	Boys	Girls	Total	Age	Approach	Teacher's Race
P.S. 40	I	10	10	20	7.7-8.5	Basal	Black
P.S. 40	II	10	10	20	6.7-8.11	Linguistic	White
P.S. 40	III	10	10	20	7.7-8.5	Basal	Black
	TOTAL	30	30	60			

Racial Background and Speech Patterns of Teachers and Researcher

The design of the research was to enable the researcher to capture the dialect speech of the subjects. In order to assure these youngsters that it was an alright "thing" to use dialect, the researcher decided to communicate in the dialect of the children. This was possible because the researcher had the facility of both standard English and Black dialect speech. The researcher was Black and had grown up in a neighborhood quite similar to that of the subjects used in this study. The ability to converse with the subjects in a style with which they were familiar enabled the subjects to engage in a free flowing conversation which otherwise might not have been possible.

The two teachers using the Basal reader approach were Black and generally used standard speech in the classroom. They were, however, thoroughly able to understand the dialect of the children. Dialect speech was corrected in some manner daily, making the child aware that standard English was desired. The teacher of the third group was white and spoke no dialect to the children. Once again, dialect speech was corrected daily. These teachers were all extremely sensitive to children's needs and the attempted shifts from dialect speech to standard English were made in subtle and positive ways without crudely indicating to the child that his dialect was not preferred.

Selection of Words

Some of the words selected for investigation in this study were exactly those cited by Labov (1969) as words which many Black urban school children pronounce phonologically differently. Other words chosen were words listed in the back of second grade readers used by children participating in this study. A word list was constructed with at least three representative words of each phonological characteristic identified by Labov as being dialectal.

The following list of words was given to teachers who were asked to have children become familiar with them on an informal basis. This list of words was distributed to three teachers of second grade at least two months prior to the researchers first visit to the school. The teachers were asked to do two things.

1. Identify with a check mark the words with which children have a passing familiarity.

2. Have the children become familiar with the other words, using an informal classroom technique.

The researcher recommended use of the listed words in writing experience charts and original stories. The actual words used in the present study were drawn from this list of words. The final selection was made on the basis of number of words familiar to the largest number of children in the three classes (see Table 3).

Design of Study

This was essentially a three-part study designed to test two hypotheses.

I. A Three Part Study

Part one used a picture folder in order to elicit speech patterns of the children through conversation. This established dialect and standard speech of words chosen for study.

In part two, each child was asked to listen to taped episodes presented in dialect and in standard English and to state in each case which one he thought was "right."

Part three presented the child with three word recognition sheets containing pictures of common objects and events. Each picture was accompanied by the name of the picture, which was printed in both standard and dialect orthography.

II. Materials

A. Picture Folder

The picture folder was a six-sided fold-out consisting of 14 brightly colored pictures (see Appendix B for pictures used). Each picture represented a word chosen whose possible pronunciation could be characteristic of Black English. These were the same characteristics examined in part two, the taped episodes, and in part three on the word recognition sheets. The children's responses were taped and hand recorded on a recording sheet.

Table 3

List From Which Words Were Chosen for Part
One, Two and Three and Phonological Characteristic Studied

Phonological Characteristic	Word
Medial "th" sound	mother father brother bathroom
Initial "th" sound	they that them there
Final "th" sound	mouth breath teeth both
"r" lessness	four star car for hard park
"l" lessness	help children tool shovel

Table 3 (continued)

Phonological Characteristic	Word
Simplification of consonant clusters	lift children wind friend blowing playing scrubbing cleaning
Use of "es" for plurals	desks tests masks ghosts
Other phonological variables	pail - pill pin - pen pitcher - picture

The picture layout was as follows:

Page	Characteristic	Picture
1	medial "th"	mother and father
1	"r" lessness	car
2	"r" lessness	numbers up to four
2	simplification of consonant cluster	children playing
3	"l" lessness	tools
3	simplification of consonant cluster	woman washing or scrubbing the floor
4	substitution of final "th"	mouth, with teeth showing

Page	Characteristic	Picture
4	substitution of final "th"	child taking a bath
5	use of "es" for plurals	ghosts masks
6	other phonological variables	pitcher picture
6	other phonological variables	potato being peeled and water pail

B. Taped Episodes on Cassette

There were 13 episodes representing the same characteristics on tape. The episodes were written by two Black children, ages 8 and 9. They also provided the actual voices heard on the tape. Both children alternated using dialect and standard English, preventing the possibility of a fixed pattern of speech for either child, which might have interfered with the subject's selection of dialect or standard English choice of words. The episodes were designed so that sometimes dialect speech was presented as preferred and at other times standard English was presented as a preference. Subject's responses were hand recorded from cassette tape. The taped episodes were as follows:

1. Episode one: Focus on r-lessness

    a. My lil brother is foh years old.

    b. He's not foh, he's four.

    a. Thas what I said.

2. Focus on use of "es" for plural

    a. Mike, we had two tesses today and I passed both of them.

b. I don't believe you passed both of them, anyway it <u>tests</u>.

3. <u>Focus on final "th"</u>

   a. You have dirty <u>teeth</u>.

   b. No I don't, and you telling me about bad speech, it's <u>teef</u>.

4. <u>Focus on medial "th"</u>

   a. My <u>movah</u> better than your <u>movah</u>.

   b. She is not.

   a. She is too, wanna bet.

   b. Yeah! And it's not <u>movah</u>, it's <u>mother</u>.

5. Focus on final "th"

   a. You have a big <u>mouth</u>.

   b. So do you.

   a. Oh shut up.

   b. No stupid, your whole family got a big <u>mouf</u>.

6. <u>Focus on use of "es" for plurals</u>

   a. We got 24 new <u>desses</u> in our classroom.

   b. So, we have 30 new <u>desks</u> in our classroom.

7. <u>Focus on final "th"</u>

   a. Hurry up, I wanna take a <u>baff</u>.

   b. Would you stop saying <u>baff</u> and say <u>bath</u>.

8. <u>Focus on simplification of consonant clusters</u>

   a. Can you <u>liff</u> me up?

   b. Nope.

   a. Why not?

   b. Because I don't watn to, and if you want to talk to me, please say <u>lift</u>.

9. <u>Focus on 1-lessness</u>

    a. If you were drowning, what would you say?

    b. I'd say <u>hepp</u> me, <u>hepp</u> me!

    a. No you wouldn't.

    b. Then what would I say?

    a. You'd say <u>help</u> me! <u>Help</u> me!

10. <u>Focus on initial "th"</u>

    a. Hurry up, <u>dey</u> goin to the circus.

    b. What did you say?

    a. I say, <u>dey</u> goin to the circus.

    b. You must mean, <u>they</u> are going to the circus.

11. <u>Focus on other phonological variables</u>

    a. Do I have to write with a <u>pin</u>?

    b. No you have to write with a <u>pen</u>.

12. <u>Focus on other phonological variables</u>

    a. Hang my <u>picture</u> right here.

    b. You say dat funny. I say <u>picha</u>.

13. <u>Focus on simplification of consonant clusters</u>

    a. Da <u>win</u> be <u>blowin</u> dem clothese out dere.

    b. Do you mean that <u>wind</u> is <u>blowing</u> those clothes out there?

C. Word Recognition Sheet

There were three word recognition sheets consisting of 13 words in standard English, 13 words representing a dialect version of those words and 13 pictures. The pictures were placed between two columns of words representing standard and dialect orthography. The pictures were clearly drawn and words were printed in manuscript for the purpose of easy reading. The dialect orthography was randomly assigned to columns to minimize position effects (see Appendix C).

The layout of the word recognition sheets was as follows:

Page	Standard English Word	Picture	Dialect Word
1	four	4	foh
1	car	car	caa
1	help	2 children with hands up in water	hepp
1	tools	picture of tools	toos
2	pin	safety pin	pen
2	blowing	clothes blowing on a line	blowin
2	children	children playing	chirren
2	mouth	mouth and teeth	mouf
2	teeth	mouth and teeth	teef
3	wind	man's hat blowing off	winn
3	pen	ball point pen	pin
3	desks	2 desks	desses
3	mother	mother's face	movah

D. Recording Sheet

Each recording sheet contained space for the child's name, age, grade, school and date (see Appendix A). Information recorded on this sheet was obtained from:

    1. picture folder

2. cassette recording

3. word recognition sheet

III. Procedure

On the day the research was to be conducted the researcher went to the class containing the first group of second graders who were to participate in the study. The classroom teacher, a young Black female introduced the researcher to the children, explaining to them that some of the children would be asked to accompany the researcher to the "family room." She explained that the researcher would tell each child what he was expected to do when working in the "family room." The reseacher took one child at a time into a room designated as the "family room" in the public school. This room is set aside for parents to use for their own purposes. The bright curtains and posters helped in creating a pleasant environment. The family room was furnished with a couch and upholstered chair, book cases, two sewing machines and a cluster of adult sized tables and chairs. A child sized table and two small chairs were brought into the room for the purpose of conducting the research. The tape recorder, microphone and picture folder were displayed on the table in readiness. On a table next to this table, were all the other instruments necessary in carrying out the study; the dialect tape, the word recognition sheets, response sheets and pencils. The researcher told each child that she wanted him to tell her about the pictures in the picture folder, listen to a tape, answer some questions about them, and work on the word recognition sheets provided. There was some open discussion about school and the tape recorder in order to put the child at ease and establish rapport. After a few minutes the child was asked to take a pencil and fill in the information on the bottom of the recording sheet; his name, birth date, class and date.

43

The researcher then opened the picture folder and showed the child the pictures. In this component of the research the researcher was looking for the pronunciation of the words listed in part "A" of the recording sheet. The response of dialect speech was recorded on the recording sheet as well as on tape. The information received from the subject's discussion of the pictures provided the pronunciation of the words the researcher wanted to examine from each subject.

The researcher then introduced the second part of the study to the child. In this part the child was asked to place a value judgment on the speech patterns he heard on tape. The researcher asked the child to listen to several short episodes on tape where words were pronounced in dialect and standard English, and to tell the researcher which of the pronunciations he heard were "right." The tape recorder was turned on, and the child listened to one short episode. The tape recorder was stopped at the end of one segment, and the researcher said, for example, "Michael said 'foah,' Gregory said 'four,' you be the judge, which one you think be sayin it right?"

The subject's response provided basically three possible pieces of information:

1. The child hears no difference between dialect and standard English.

2. The child hears a distinction between dialect speech and standard English.

3. The child is able to make a judgment and gives a preference as to which speech pattern he feels is "right."

The researcher indicated the subject's choice on the recording sheet by putting a circle around the preferred version of the word.

In the third part of the study, the child is presented with three word recognition sheets. Each child was asked to write his name on the top of the first page. He was then asked to look at the pictures and then at the words. Next, the child was asked to "find the word that you think goes with the picture. Draw a circle around that word." The child's selection indicated whether or not he preferred traditional to dialect orthography.

CHAPTER IV

RESULTS AND CONCLUSIONS

This study dealt with the identification of phonological characteristics of dialect speech of Black second grade children, of low socio-economic
background in New York City Public Schools. ✻There were two hypotheses investigated in the study. First, there is a positive correlation between incidence
of dialect speech of Black second graders and their perception that dialect
speech is bad, and second, use of dialect speech does not interfere with the
dialect speaker's ability to identify words in traditional orthography. A
positive correlation was hypothesized based on the notion that dialect speaking
children in school would already have received sufficient "correction" of
their speech to perceive that their speech was "bad." Type of materials used
for reading instruction were also examined as a variable. Data to test these
hypotheses was gathered from the following tasks:

Part I (S) - Dialect speaking: This task measured the
number of pronunciations in dialect of 18
words used in describing pictures from a
picture folder.

Part II (P) - To examine the perception that dialect speech
is "bad." Alternative pronunciations of 14

words were presented and the number of
standard English choices were scored.

Part III (P) - A task involving identification of words
written in both tranditional orthography
and dialect was presented and the number
of standard English choices from 13 pairs
of presented words was scored.

The histograms demonstrate the incidence of dialect speech (as measured on the test) drawn from each class and the total group. A visual inspection of each histogram indicates a relatively unskewed distribution of scores. Therefore, the assumption of normal distribution could be made and parametric tests were used to test the hypotheses.

Figure 1 indicates four children in Class I used 7-11 incidents of dialect speech, nine children used 12-14 incidents of dialect speech, and seven children used 16-17 incidents of dialect speech. Figures 2 and 3 also provide a graphic picture of dialect usage in terms of scores from 1-18. It is clearly illustrated that dialect speech of Class II is more spread out; less dense, than dialect speech classes I and III. The minimum score of dialect usage for Class I was seven incidences, whereas the minimum score for Class II was one incidence, and the minimum for Class III was a score of six incidences of dialect speech.

Figures 4, 5, and 6 represent histograms showing preferences for dialect speech when heard with standard English. Class I provides the most dense scoring between one and five. Class III shows 13 children scoring between one and five incidences of dialect speech, and Class II indicates its

47

Figure 1
Incidences of Dialect Speech for Class I (Verbal)

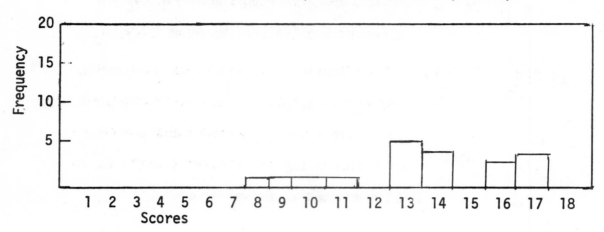

Figure 2
Incidences of Dialect Speech for Class II (Verbal)

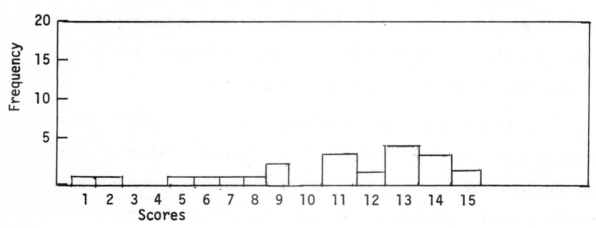

Figure 3
Incidences of Dialect Speech for Class III (Verbal)

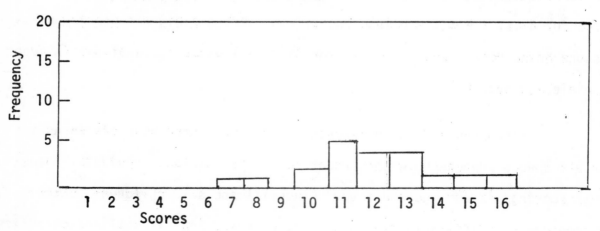

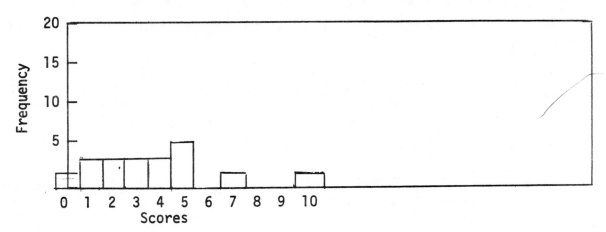

Figure 4
Incidences of Dialect Speech for Class I (Auditory)

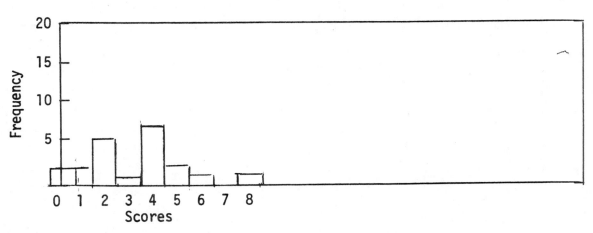

Figure 5
Incidences of Dialect Speech for Class II (Auditory)

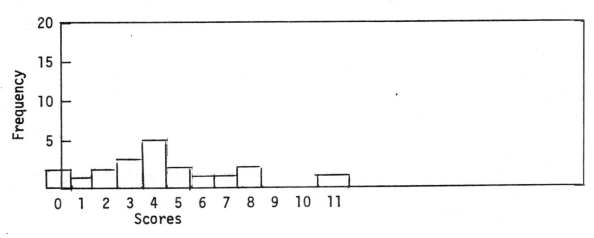

Figure 6
Incidences of Dialect Speech for Class III (Auditory)

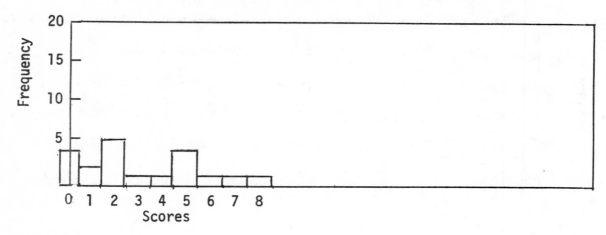

Figure 7
Incidences of Dialect Speech for Class I (Visual)

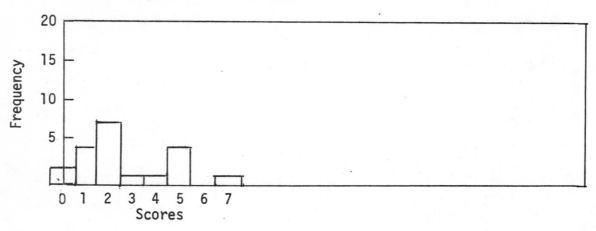

Figure 8
Incidences of Dialect Speech for Class II (Visual)

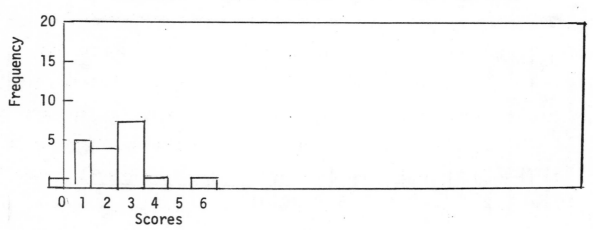

Figure 9
Incidences of Dialect Speech for Class III (Visual)

heaviest dialect preference at scores of two and four.

The figures 7, 8, and 9 show histograms representing dialect choices of written words then paired with traditional orthography. Class I shows heavy dialect concentration around scores of two and five incidences, including 13 children. Class II has its heaviest concentration at scoring points one, two and five incidences, which includes 15 children. Class III indicates heavy incidences of dialect speech between scores of one, two and three representing 17 children.

Figure 10 indicates the mean incidence of dialect speech of the three classes on the three parts of the test. One can readily see the high use of dialect speech in all three classes.

Table 4 illustrates the percent of the total number of students in each class that showed evidence of dialect-speech characteristics in three ways; verbal evidence, preference for dialect speech, and identification of dialect in written form. It is clearly seen that the phonological characteristics noted as simplification of consonant clusters, substitution of final "th," and other phonological variables are the most prevalent dialect speech characteristics in all three classes; scoring above 90 percent usage. Most of the dialect speech characteristics which receive zero percent, were located in the "P" column, indicating dialect preference. It reads, no one in Class I showed a preference for dialect speech in the categories of 1-lessness, and substitution of initial and medial "th." In Class II no one, or zero percent showed preference for r-lessness, 1-lessness, and substitution of initial "th." In Class III everyone showed evidence of dialect speech preference, ranging from 5-90 percent. In Class I, intra-class percentages sometimes were

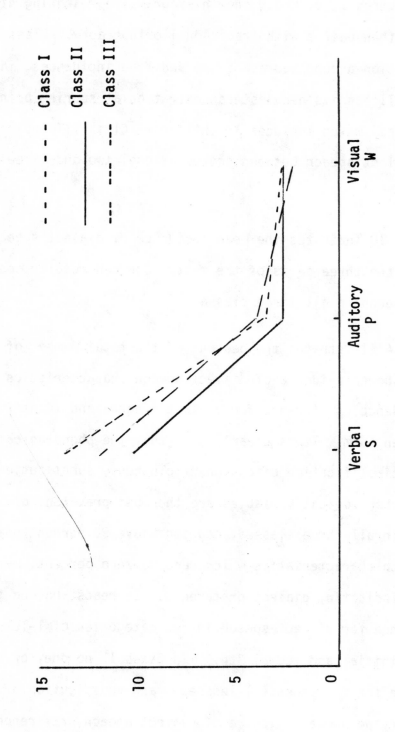

Figure 10

Mean Dialect Speech on Part I, II, and III for
Individual Classes

Class I

Class II

Class III

Table 4

Percent of Students in Each Class with Specified Dialect Speech Characteristics

Characteristics	Class I			Class II			Class III		
	S*	P*	W*	S	P	W	S	P	W
Sub. med "th"	45	0	5	45	10	5	40	5	0
Other phon. var.	100	80	60	100	85	65	95	90	70
r-lessness	95	5	15	80	0	0	85	10	5
l-lessness	95	0	35	75	0	20	90	20	20
Sub. initial "th"	100	0	**	60	0	**	60	5	**
Simp. of consonant cluster	100	45	45	90	35	-55	100	55	20
Sub. of final "th"	95	45	50	90	50	45	95	35	40
Uses of "es for plurals	85	55	30	70	65	35	90	60	50

* S = Speech; P = Perception; W = Words

** There was no sub. initial "th" on the visual test.

extremely striking, with Class I indicating 100 percent verbal dialect characteristics in the category of substitution of initial "th," 95 percent l-lessness and zero percent preference for dialect speech in those same areas. R-lessness almost falls in the same category, with 95 percent of the children in Class I showing evidence of having that characteristic, and only five percent of children showing preference for its use. Another interesting statistic is in Class II with the characteristic r-lessness, where 80 percent of the children showed usage, none showed a preference for that characteristic, and no one selected it in the word identification part of the study. A statistical analysis of these percentages and their correlations is presented below.

Table 5 shows total number of children and percent of specified dialect speech characteristics. These numbers and percents are representative of the three parts of the tasks and are results of scores obtained to test the hypotheses. The first hypothesis states that there is a positive correlation between the incidence of dialect speech and the child's perception that dialect speech is bad. The measure of dialect speech is Part I, and the measure of the perception of dialect speech is Part II (the perception that dialect speech is bad if defined as a high standard English score on the auditory test).

To test this hypothesis the Pearson Product Moment Correlation was used with 95 percent confidence intervals on ρ (rho). The correlations computed on all three classes as well as the overall correlation came out negative (see Table 6). This meant that the higher the dialect speaking score the lower the preference for standard English on the auditory perception test, Part II. The more children tended to speak dialect, the more they perceived it as being "right." Therefore, for Classes I and II there was a statistically significant correlation between dialect speech and perception of dialect speech.

Table 5

Total Number and Percent of Children in Three Classes With Specified Dialect Speech Characteristics

Characteristics	S*		P*		W*	
	N	%	N	%	N	%
Sub. medial "th"	26	43	3	05	2	03
Other phon. var.	59	98	51	85	39	65
r-lessness	52	87	3	05	4	07
l-lessness	52	87	4	07	15	25
Sub. initial "th"	44	73	1	02	**	
Simp. of consonant cluster	58	97	27	45	24	40
Sub. of final "th"	56	93	26	43	27	45
Uses of "es" for plurals	53	88	36	60	23	38

* S = Speech; P = perception; W = Words

** There was no substitution of initial "th" on the word recognition test. There are 60 children in all three classes combined.

Table 6

Results of Correlation for Individual Classes and
Overall for Hypothesis I

Class	Correlation	t
Class I	R = -.5262	-3.0873*
Class II	R = -.7684	-7.9598*
Class III	R = -.2789	-1.2831
Overall	R = -.4851	-4.8313*

* $p < .05$

This was a negative correlation, indicating that the higher the dialect speech score, the lower the standard English score. In the third class the correlation was negative, although not statistically significant. The trend, however, was clear.

These results fail to confirm the hypothesis that there is a positive correlation between dialect speaking, and perception that dialect speaking is bad.

The second hypothesis states that dialect speech is not related to the identification of written words. A Pearson Product Moment Correlation was also used to test this hypothesis. The measure of dialect speech was derived from Part I, and the measure of the identification of written words from Part III. The correlation computed on all three classes as well as the overall correlation was negative. Although the difference was not in direction expected, the null hypothesis was not rejected because the correlations were not statistically significant.

Table 7 illustrates the correlation for each class as well as the overall correlation for hypothesis II.

Table 7

Results of Correlation for Individual Classes and
Overall for Hypothesis II

Class	Correlation
I	R = -.1320
II	R = -.2763
III	R = .0178
Overall	R = -.1928

Inspecting the confidence interval for the correlation over all three classes we see that on the negative side that 18 percent of the variance is explained by the linear relationship, this percentage being quite small; on the positive side only a fraction, 36 percent of the variance, is explained by the linear relationship. Thus, the conclusion can be drawn with some degree of confidence that there is no relationship between dialect speech and the identification of the written word. If, as found, there is no relationship, this finding between dialect speech and identification of the written word, then we can infer that dialect speech does not interfere with the child's ability to identify the word in traditional orthography.

In addition to testing two hypotheses, the study considered the reading approach being used in a class, as two of the classes, I and III, were using a Basal reader approach, and the third class, Class II, used a linguistic approach to reading. An analysis of variance was used to determine if there were any significant differences between the three classes in incidence of dialect speech.

The measure used for dialect speech was Part I; ANOVA yielded an F of 5.80, significant at $p < .05$. Thus the conclusion can be made that there was a significant difference in the means of the three classes. See Table 8.

Table 8

Analysis of Variance Among Reading Groups

Source	D.F.	Sum of Squares	Mean Square	F
Between Groups	2	115.9	57.95	5.80
Within Groups	57	569.7	9.99	
Total	59	685.6		

F. RATIO
Significant at .05 level.

Since the F ratio was significant; contrasts, or multiple comparisons were made to determine where the actual differences were among the classes.

In order to do this, four contrasts of interest were set up:

$\hat{\Theta}_1 = \overline{X}_1 - \overline{X}_2 = 3.4$ (Class I's Dialect Speech vs. Class II's Dialect Speech)

$\hat{\Theta}_2 = \overline{X}_1 - \overline{X}_3 = 1.85$ (Class I's Dialect Speech vs. Class III's Dialect Speech)

$\hat{\Theta}_3 = \overline{X}_2 - \overline{X}_3 = -1.55$ (Class II's Dialect Speech vs. Class III's Dialect Speech)

$\hat{\Theta}_4 = \overline{X}_2 - \frac{1}{2}(\overline{X}_1 + M_3) = -2.47$ (Linguistic approach vs. Basal Reader approach)

The last contrast indicated clearly that the linguistic group seemed to have children with less dialect speech. It is entirely possible that the linguistic approach does not accentuate the conflict points in dialect speech. The interval was a negative one, indicating the average mean dialect score of Classes I and III, was significantly higher than the mean dialect score of Class II.

An alternative explanation would be that the children in Class II may have had less dialect speech <u>before</u> entering the class, and that the linguistic approach did not influence use of dialect. Although different approaches were purported to be used, we are not positive of what really transpired in the classroom.

CHAPTER V

DISCUSSION AND SOME IMPLICATIONS

If advances are to be made in the study of Black dialect as it relates to reading, then educators and linguists must continue to research and investigate every aspect of the problem. This investigation dealt with two major questions relating to dialect speech and reading skills. The first question was concerned with the Black child's dialect speech and his perception of dialect speech. The second addressed itself to dialect speech as it relates to the child's ability to identify words spelled in a traditional manner. In addition, differences in dialect speech with groups of children using different reading approaches were examined. The study specifically examined the following two hypotheses: (1) there is a positive correlation between dialect speech of Black second graders and their perception that dialect speech is bad, and (2) use of dialect speech does not interfere with the dialect speaker's ability to identify words in traditional orthography.

The phonological characteristics found in the speech of the 60 subjects investigated in this study overwhelmingly support the findings in studies conducted by Labov (1967b), Baratz (1969), Bailey (1969), and Stewart (1969). All the children tested for phonological variations showed evidence of some dialect speech. More than 50 percent of the subjects used dialect speech more than half the time, as evidenced through conversation about the pictures presented. These findings had been anticipated, due to the fact that the school was located in the heart of a dialect speaking community.

The first hypothesis, which stated there was a positive correlation between dialect speech and the child's perception that dialect speech is bad, was not substantiated. When the children were presented with samples of standard English, and dialect speech and asked, "Which one you think, say it right," the findings indicated a preference for dialect speech.

The second hypothesis, that dialect speech does not interfere with the child's ability to identify words in traditional orthography, was supported by the findings. Even though dialect speaking children perceived their dialect speech as "right," they were indeed able to identify words spelled in traditional orthography when these words were placed alongside of words spelled in dialect. This finding has significant implications for reading instruction. It strongly suggests that children who were believed by some to be severely handicapped by their dialect speech, are not impeded by dialect in learning to read.

Some additional information was generated through the investigation. In this study, the children who used the linguistic approach to reading had less dialect speech than children taught through the Basal reader approach. The reason for this difference is not at all clear and it is entirely possible that the children in this group had relatively low dialect speech characteristics to begin with, and that this finding tells us nothing about their so-called linguistic approach. This is indeed an area which should be studied.

The previous statements merely serve to bring the hypotheses and their results into focus. The remainder of this chapter will be a discussion of what these findings mean, how they relate to previous findings, and what the implications are thereof.

Discussion in Dialect Speech and Perception of Dialect

This study indicated clearly that given a similar situation the children will probably have the speech characteristics reported by Labov (1967b), Stewart (1969), Bailey (1969), and Baratz (1969). Black English as reported by Black and white researchers, does exist! However, that really is just about the extent of the commonality between this work and those studies previously cited. It appears to this researcher that a tremendous amount of additional research is needed before one ought to make the broad assumptions which are frequently made in the field of Black dialect and reading.*Many of the assumptions made about dialect speech relate use of phonological variations with the child's inability to acquire many of the skills necessary in learning to read. (The phonological characteristics discussed can be found in Appendix A, listed on the recording sheet.)

A sizable number of teachers, both Black and white refuse to acknowledge that the speech of some Black children is in fact a legitimate language and a viable means of communication for those who speak it. Instead, they prefer to classify it as "lazy," "sloppy," "incorrect" English. As cited earlier, Dillard (1972) maintains that to adhere to this idea is ridiculous. He feels there can be no effective teaching or learning if teachers remain locked in their own language modes. Similarly, white and Black linguists feel that teachers must become aware of the phonological variations as language

63

differences and not deficits. Baratz (1971) feels that negative teacher attitudes have fostered negative attitudes about reading, which have led to failure for the children concerned. Stewart (1969) and Baratz (1969) have both suggested use of dialect texts in teaching Black dialect speaking children to read. Bailey (1968) recommended teaching dialect speaking children to speak standard English prior to teaching them to read, in order to reduce the conflict. The present study advocates that teachers require thorough knowledge of the phonological variations in order to differentiate between variations and errors. The teacher's ability to hear the differences and similarities might be all that is necessary, provided there is a genuine openness and sensitivity about the child's perception of his own language. The dialect-speaking child's perception of dialect speech is an important factor to consider. Labov et al (1965) and Leaverton and Gladney (1968) showed little concern with how the child felt about his dialect speech. Baratz (1971) talked about developing a feeling of self worth in dialect speaking children, but her studies indicate minimal focus on the feelings of these children and attitudes about their dialect speech.

In the present study, it was hypothesized that there was a positive correlation between dialect speech and the child's perception that dialect was bad. The findings show that there is a correlation between dialect speech and the child's perception of his dialect speech but, in the opposite direction expected. Instead of demonstrating negative attitudes toward dialect speech, the children indicated a preference for it. In short, the dialect speaking children tested considered their language viable, and really believed in it. This investigation indicated that Black children perceive their dialect speech as "right," and therefore feel positive about the way they talk.

For teachers of primary school age children, this might mean a complete "about face" in terms of attitude. The Chicago study conducted by Leaverton and Gladney (1968), stated that teachers were constantly correcting children. Although Leaverton and Gladney (1968) suggested that he did not want to infer to the children that certain language usage was "correct" or "incorrect," he became quite involved in deciding that "at home talk" had its place and "school talk" had another place. In order to keep them separate, he had the children practice regularly, changing "at home talk" into "school talk." These exercises had to communicate something to the child in terms of attitudes about "at home talk," expressed by the teacher or researcher. This observation is not intended to criticize, but rather to point out that the Leaverton team apparently made such a point of not focusing on "correct" or "incorrect" speech to the dialect speaking child, that indeed, that is precisely what they did. Perhaps it would have been more appropriate to level with the child and say, "You need standard English in order to function in, and communicate with those in the mainstream of society."

Most Black parents seem to feel quite sure that their children should learn standard English if they are to communicate with the broader speech community and be accepted in the mainstream of society. Their children need to become aware of the differences between their dialect speech, and dialects of other ethnic groups. They also must be thoroughly cognizant of the kind of speech expected of them if they are to become successful in today's world. These observations are based on data drawn from personal interviews conducted by the researcher and college students from Bank Street College of Education, in relation to what parents want the school to teach their children.

An awareness of dialect speech of Black children and the implications for teachers must begin in the early school years, because so many educators seem to consider success in school as equivalent with standard English speech. In first and second grade classes in most public schools, reading is the primary focus. Many teachers feel that success in all other areas is contingent on success in reading. *The problem is that some teachers use oral language readiness, visual discrimination and auditory perception as measured by standard English readiness tests as indices for reading readiness. There is an element of truth in many, if not all of the above statements, therefore the statements themselves do not present the problem. It is the actions taken on behalf of those statements.* The difficulty arises when educators feel that the child's verbal ability interferes with possible reading success. Additional problems occur when linguists indicate that lack of development of auditory discrimination is indicative of an inability to identify words in standard English. Based on research, some reading people disagree. Cohen and Cooper (1972) state that it is a myth that "Poor articulation contributes to auditory discrimination deficiencies and therefore to deficiencies in learning phonics skills among disadvantaged Black and Puerto Rican children (p. 43)."

* Findings of this study indicated that dialect speech was not related to identification of the written word. Therefore, whether teachers feel that children with dialect speech can manage standard phonological sounds or not, there is little relationship between the Black child's ability to make standard English phonological sounds and the ability to read. This too is supported by Cohen and Cooper (1972). They emphasize that *changing a child's oral language pattern will not enable him to read better. Results

of the first part of this study indicated that dialect speakers had a preference for dialect speech. Since one can be sure that teachers in general do not feel positive about dialect speech, this finding creates cause for concern. Although the hypothesis was not substantiated, the findings have real implications for teachers, for the child's positive perception of his speech will certainly clash with the teacher's desire to change his speech pattern as soon as the child enters the class.

A complete reading program was developed in Chicago around "School Talk" and "At Home Talk" without ever determining how the child perceived his dialect. It is possible that a totally different program might have evolved if Leaverton and Gladney (1968) had secured information about how the dialect speaker perceived his dialect speech.

If we are aware of how children perceive their dialect speech then we must face a problem of grave dimensions. That is, how do teachers perceive the dialect speech of Black children? Perhaps it will take years of re-education before teachers of early childhood classes begin to perceive dialect speech in a positive way. The point that needs to be emphasized is that speaking is not reading. Teachers must begin to separate language activities in terms of influential forces. Although it is true that reading and language skills are closely inter-related, success of one is not contingent on a prescribed behavior of another. For example, many excellent readers speak in non-standard English or dialect. Similarly, dialect speaking children are able to understand directions spoken in standard English well enough to complete a task (Mueser, 1971).

Perhaps the reason that educators have avoided the question of the child's perception of his language is that it relates to feelings and attitudes which are in the affective domain, and teachers tend to be more concerned with activities related to the cognitive domain. Parent worries about high reading scores, and providing children with tools necessary for moving into the mainstream of society, are absolutely legitimate. There are a variety of ways to achieve these goals.

The present study intended to imply that the way the child perceives himself and his language, in the school environment, might perhaps be more important than teaching him standard English from the first day of school. Indeed, if there was real understanding of the language of the child in light of its differences, and opportunities to use that language, positive interaction should begin between the child and teacher. When positive interaction occurs, the teacher will have an easier time teaching that child any number of things, even standard English. Stewart (1969), and Baratz (1969) advocate teaching dialect speaking children to read using dialect materials. The assumption underlying this suggestion is that it would be a more effective approach since it would be more closely related to the phonemes used by non-standard speakers. Baratz and Stewart seem to feel the discrepancy between the language of the school and the child is a cause of failure. It could be that an additional reason for suggesting such a program would be for development of positive feelings about one's language. This study pointed out that Black children already have a positive feeling about their language, and there are many ways of increasing the positive approach about one's mother tongue, short of creating dialect readers. However, a longitudinal study based on use of dialect readers may prove to be a worthwhile investigation. The findings of this study, however, indicate that it is not necessary to create material visually more related to dialect speech in order to teach the child to read.

68

This study indicated that dialect speech is not related to the child's ability to identify words in standard or traditional orthography. Confidence intervals for the correlation over all three classes indicate that only 36 percent of the variance is explained by linear relationship on the positive side, and 18 percent of the variance is explained by linear relationship on the negative side. The major portion of variance must therefore be explained in another way.

The Black children participating in the study showed indications of being a bi-dialectal group, and well able to communicate in dialect speech while addressing themselves to standard English reading material. This was evidenced by their high scores in dialect and their ability to select the correct orthography for a given word, as well as the ability to read as evidenced by the Metropolitan Achievement Test.

Joan Baratz (1969) feels that Black children are not bi-dialectal and therefore handle all verbal and reading material in a dialectal way. In her study which tested ability to recall statements in standard English she maintained that Black children transformed these sentences into dialect and were unable to recall the statements in standard English. Nolan (1972) also examined differences in the recall of printed language pattern with 156 Black and Caucasian second and fourth grade children of low socio-economic status. Standardized reading passages in standard English (S.S.E.) with equivalent forms rewritten in Black dialect and non-standardized reading passages in Black-dialect were used. Black children showed no reliable differences in performance related to language patterns. Second grade Black children's reading recall of both standardized passages and non-standard passages was not significantly different from that of Caucasian children.

Only at grade four did Caucasian children recall significantly more than their Black counterparts. There was no significant interaction between the dialect variable and race on grade of reader. The researcher, Nolan (1972) had predicted that reading language patterns similar to their own speech patterns would be significantly higher than scores of student reading and recalling material with reading patterns different from their speech. If children are feeling positive about their dialect speech and are able to recall in standard patterns of speech, then teachers can perhaps help to further develop this attitude through greater use of the child's own dialect speech. This would tend to acknowledge to the child that he has a perfectly acceptable pattern of speech even though there is another whole speech pattern which is also used in school for reading. What is important about the Baratz and Nolan study, having examined the same question, is the difference in their findings about the dialectal characteristic of Black children's speech. Other researchers have supported the Nolan study in this respect and their studies substantiate the bi-dialectal characteristics of Black children's speech (Fryburg, 1970; Nolan, 1972, and Valentine, (1971).

Teachers frequently complain that they cannot understand the speech of dialect speaking children. Rystrom and Cowart (1972) feel that a major obligation of teachers is learning to understand the dialect of children whose speech is different from their own dialect. In their study they found the race of the tester to have significant effect upon decoding scores of Black subjects. Their study did much to bring into focus the attitudes of white teachers in classrooms of Black children.

The Fleming (1970) study addresses itself to teacher attitudes and reading performance. He talks about linguistically unsophisticated teachers and how they respond to dialectal deviations as if they were reading errors. Teachers need to recognize Black dialect as a viable means of communication for Black youngsters. Hopefully this investigation of how Black children perceive their language will aid teachers in this recognition. This plea for recognition of Black dialect as a viable dialect is not by any means addressed only to white middle class teachers of Black children. Certainly, Black teachers, who think they are linguistically sophisticated, prove to be as high in percentage as whites in forming this group of the linguistically unsophisticated. To children, their attitudes about language are as "nasty" as the attitudes of whites. To be sure, this group sometimes has stronger feeling than whites about the kind of language to be accepted from Black school youngsters. The fact that one might agree with Fleming does not negate the strong desire to equip Black children with every facility with which to move into the mainstream of society and to communicate with the broader speech community. Indeed the approach of recognition of one's dialect, and acceptance of its use in the classroom might be the factor needed in facilitating standard English. The researcher conducting this study is unaware of any other studies which investigate the young Black child's perception of his dialect.

One factor which needs to be examined in terms of the children's responses, is the fact that the researcher was Black and conducted the interviews in a language style familiar to the children. The purpose of this was to encourage the children to speak in a natural, relaxed form of speech.

There is a real possibility that the dialect speech of the interviewer might in some way have influenced the responses in Part II of the study. In this part of the study the children were asked if standard English or dialect speech was "right." The children indicated dialect speech as

71

being said "right." In order to test this out, it is recommended that the study be carried out by a white investigator using standard English for the interview. It is possible that the children label the dialect "right" to avoid offending the investigator.

Although studies in language preference of young children are extremely scarce, there are a few which address this question with young adults. Work by Labov (1964) and Kaplan (1969) focus on this subject to a slight degree, with lower class Puerto Rican and Black youngsters. A preference for non-standard English was alluded to in their study. Labov and Kaplan report a polarization of linguistic attitudes in which a growing number of lower class whites, Blacks and Puerto Ricans reject speech patterns by the dominant group and adopt a speech pattern close to Southern Black dialect (Labov, 1964, pp. 96-97).

Another study with older children was conducted by Hensley and Hatch (1970). Their study investigated attitudes about Black English by Black high school youngsters. The investigation which was conducted in Los Angeles, California found that Black students were generally unfavorable to Black English.

A major focus of the present study was to attempt to find out how the Black child perceived his dialect speech. Perception here implied both the ability to discriminate between words as well as to form judgment by perceiving. Hence, the child was asked, "Which one you think be sayin' it right, you be the judge." One cannot ignore the teacher variable in the child's perception of dialect speech. Indeed it might have been interesting to ask their feelings about the teacher. The preference for Black dialect from the present subjects confirms similar indications by Blacks and Puerto

72

Ricans in Labov's work (1964). It is important to note that the researcher who conducted the present study was Black and indeed interacted with the children in a dialect speech pattern. One wonders what the results would have been if the researcher was Black using standard English, or white, using standard English? Further research would provide enlightenment in this area, and possible answer some of the questions still unanswered.

The first hypothesis of this study was not substantiated by the data. There was not a positive correlation between dialect speech and the child's perception that dialect speech was bad, but instead there was a negative correlation. The overall score for three classes, as indicated by Pearson Product Moment Correlation, was $r = -.4851$. This negative correlation indicates a preference for non-standard English or the notion that dialect speech is not bad.

What are the implications for teachers of Black children who have a preference for dialect speech? First, educators must understand that dialect speech is a viable means of communication for some Black school children. Teachers can determine speech patterns through tasks similar to those used in this investigation. If findings are similar, one can then assume that the children tested have the ability to discriminate between dialect speech and standard English. Second, the language of Black children will probably be perpetuated as long as they reside in a dialect speaking community. Therefore these children will continue to bring dialect speech into the classroom. It must be remembered, however, that Black dialect speaking children can handle both patterns of speech, since they are or will become bi-dialectal. Philosophically, it's somewhat similar to W. E. B. DuBois' point of view discussed in Souls of Black Folk (1903). This point was that Black folks indeed have two souls; one Black and one American. Similarly, Black children today operate in two worlds of speech; one white and one Black. It is for this reason precisely that schools must accept a dual speech approach and not allow the dialect speech of a child to hinder possible progress in reading. Since there is more than an indication that the children can handle the language differences, there should be a plea for teachers to begin to do the same.

Another area where dialect speaking children have less difficulty in terms of interference than teachers seem to feel they have, is the area of word identification in traditional orthography.

Discussion on Dialect Speech and Orthography

The findings in this investigation clearly illustrate that the child's dialect speech does not interfere with his ability to identify words written in traditional orthography. Another way of stating this is that dialect speech is apparently not related to the identification of the traditionally written word. Investigation of dialect scores and their relationship to traditional orthography indicate a relationship $r = -.1370$ for Class I, $1 = -.2763$ for Class II, and $r = -.0178$ for Class III. Inspection of the confidence intervals for the correlation over all three classes shows only 36 percent of the variance is explained by the linear relationship.

Orthography means correct spelling. Correct spelling to educators and teachers is spelling that is accepted as standard by the educated population of the world. In the present study there was no focus on how the child actually encoded or spelled the word, but rather, his ability to identify the traditionally spelled word when placed next to the same word spelled in dialect.

74

This skill would relate to the decoding skills required in reading. The findings or results supported the stated hypothesis and confirmed findings in much of the previous literature. The Kligman (1972) study indicated that although there were dialect related errors in the spelling performance of Black children, white children made some of the same errors that Black children made. His findings emphasize clearly that in the dialect speech-spelling relationship, only selected features caused enough difficulty for one to become concerned. Clearly then, one can see, if there is not enough dialect related spelling difficulty evidenced to cause concern, then the focus of the classroom teachers should probably be on errors commonly made by white and Black children alike. Two different channels of communication are used for spelling and reading. Spelling involves an encoding process, whereas reading is a process of decoding. The present study and the Kligman study are related, but deal with different channels of communication.

Some very interesting observations were made while collecting these data used in the investigation, which might relate to the child's process of arriving at choices made. Some of the children went through a verbal process which seemed to clarify for the researcher a possible approach used frequently in similar situations.

One subject looked at the picture of two desks on page three of the word recognition sheet. She then proceeded to look at the words, "desks" and "desses." She said to herself, while pointing to the word desks, "desses," you know desses don got no two s's." This youngster then marked the word "desks" as the correct word to go with the picture of two desks. This is a clear illustration of the child's verbal response to two desks, as desses, but demonstrates no confusion in the way the word was spelled traditionally.

One can never really say there is absolutely no relationship since the statistical findings were not zero. However, one can conclude from our findings that the relationship if any is not statistically significant and certainly not pedagogically significant. Stewart (1971) makes it clear that he feels there is interference when he states:

> ...if the differences (between SE and NNE phonology) are regular enough, which they often are, then the Negro dialect speaker may be able to set up his own sound-spelling correspondences between them--one which will be different from those set up by a speaker of SE, but will allow effective word identification nevertheless (p. 3).

The present study indicates no need for formalizing such a procedure. The children seem to be coping on their own. Creating a program of sound-spelling correspondence especially for Black dialect speaking children would tend to be extremely confusing. Baratz (1971) advocates construction of a phonics program that makes the sound-spelling correspondence between standard English orthography and Black English phonology explicit for the child. The present study does not support this approach.

If these changes were advocated for everyone on the basis of irregularities in our spelling system then the element of confusion would equally apply to all. Indeed, spelling would perhaps be a simple routine for everyone because there would be a close phoneme-grapheme relationship. But to consider such a proposal for Black dialect speaking children only, would produce utter confusion for the dialect speaking child. He would indeed have his dialect, standard English, traditional orthography as well as the proposed dialect spelling to contend with. This kind of confusion would conceivably affect the child's total progress in reading more than any other single factor.

To gain knowledge in the area of orthography, one needs to investigate carefully the opinion of the authorities or experts in this field.

On the question of linguistics and spelling, Venezky (1970) feels that the most important data the linguist can provide are those which relate to (a) pronunciation, (b) the writing system, and (c) the relationship between speech and writing. He emphasizes that our spelling program is irregular and therefore sometimes irrational. However, it is the accepted spelling program by the educated group and considered standard English orthography. Teachers know there is slight relationship, but since it is not statistically significant there is no need to assume the performance in one area is a predictor of performance in another area. In essence, what this actually says is that dialect speech is not an indicator that the youngster will perform poorly on word identification skills.

One could ask at this point, if the reading scores are lower with Black dialect speaking children and these data collected do not indicate cause for reading failure, then what does? Two factors should be considered as possibly relating to the overall poor reading performance. First, the question of teacher attitudes needs to be taken into consideration, and second the type of reading program must be studied as a related factor in poor reading performance. The subjects examined in this study were involved in two reading approaches, Basal reader and linguistic. Even in the Basal reading group phonics was used as a method of teaching skills to those children. We need to consider all possible phonological differences before choosing an approach to teaching dialect speaking children to read. Did the particular phonetic approach used possibly accentuate the conflict areas in the phonology of Black dialect speech? Did the linguistic approach used in some way elude those conflict areas? The answers to these questions would require a thorough examination of the reader's materials and strategies, which is outside the scope of this investigation.

MacGinitie (1965) feels that linguistics as a science has made a contribution to the field of reading. He stated:

> The contribution of linguistics to reading has thus far been primarily in the area of phonology, that is, the sound system of the language. Those who have, in the past, advocated a strong emphasis on "phonics" in the teaching of reading had had their arguments countered by illustrations of irregularities in the way the sound system is rendered into print. Linguists have made, and are continuing to make, studies of the grapheme-phoneme correspondence that do exist in English. As a result of these studies, it is possible to prepare reading materials in which these correspondences are reasonably simple and uniform, thus simplifying the task of learning these correspondences for the beginning reader.

McGinitie makes it clear, however, that the assumption should not be made that all the problems of reading instruction will be solved by the use of the linguistic approach in reading.

Similar feelings about linguistics and reading are discussed by Wardhaugh (1969) and he indicates that the problem in initial reading instruction is partly one of showing the child how the relationship of the marks he sees on paper to sounds that come out of peoples' mouths. He also feels that current linguistic knowledge should enable teachers to build on the child's capabilities by making the child's task as simple as possible. Knowledge of linguistics in general should assist the teacher in exactly what phonological variation Black speakers use. It is then necessary for teachers to know precisely which of these variations are used by particular children in his or her class.

It can be said with some degree of certainty that Black parents and Black and white teachers all want the child to ultimately learn standard English. It is the teacher's responsibility to help each child to develop the ability to select the appropriate usage for certain situations. This would provide the child with the power of choice to decide for himself what usage is appropriate on the basis of purpose, meaning, and effect he desires the communication to produce.

There are still more questions than answers in reference to the effect dialect usage will have on beginning reading. Therefore, continued research is absolutely essential in this area.

Recommendations for Teachers of Black Dialect Speaking Children

The development of language is a natural outgrowth of the living process and is directly related to one's life style, beliefs and experience. The teacher needs to know the qualities and structure of the language spoken in the community, as well as the language of each child in order to foster open communication and to assist the child in moving to universal speech patterns. Therefore each teacher should be able to identify the dialect of a community and assess the way it affects the lexical and phonemic characteristics of the members of that entire community.

The child's dialect speech is perpetuated through other children in the community. The teacher needs to be aware of the lexical choices of the child as well as the phonology he uses in formulating these words used in school. A thorough understanding of the child's oral speech pattern is necessary in order for the teacher to develop or select effective reading programs. It is absolutely necessary for the teacher to have the ability and tools to identify the dialect speech of Black school children, and children should be taught to discriminate between the differences in his language pattern and standard English. These differences should be emphasized in positive ways which do not undermine the child's own language.

In order for the child to have effective communication with the broader speech community, he needs to be guided in communicative ideas under varied circumstances. The teacher needs to aid the child whose dialect restricts his communication process to expand his linguistic skills so that he gains a larger measure of control over his social environment. Therefore, the teacher should be able to move the child from his dialect speech to a universal speech pattern.

The tasks used in this study have proven to be quite reliable. Statisticians (Davis, 1965) note that for measuring the average characteristics for groups reliability coefficients as low as .50 is considered highly reliable (p. 24). The range for these original instruments used for this study was from .55 to .75. Instruments such as these could be used by researchers from any ethnic group, working with dialect speaking children. It should also prove interesting to do a study using these materials with Black and white children.

Limitations of Present Study

One of the major limitations of the present study is that the investigator had no real way of knowing the effect of her presence on the responses of the children. In order to produce results which attempt to control this variable it would be necessary to use investigators of different ethnic and language background or design a test in which data gathering was completely automated. Comparisons would then be made in an attempt to see the effect of the stated variable.

Another limitation of the investigation was that no hypothesis was made in reference to various reading approaches, as they relate to Black dialect speech. In order for this to be accomplished, large numbers of classes of children randomly assigned to different approaches would be needed.

Despite these limitations, however, this study did illuminate a small part of the Black dialect-beginning reading question. The data show that the Black child, even though he may use Black dialect and even though he may express preference for Black dialect, when presented with spoken choices, can, when required to choose between a printed rendering of Black dialect and standard English orthography, choose correctly. It is this finding that has implications for the reading instruction of Black children. Black dialect speaking children can be taught to read standard English orthography without changing their spoken language patterns.

Recommendations for Further Research

If progress is to be made in study of reading as it relates to dialect speaking children, researchers must continue to investigate all factors which seem to contribute to the problem. However, the research is useless unless teachers read, assess, and utilize the findings applicable to their classroom population. In order to make sound decisions it is imperative to study and evaluate all of the research; that which opposes use of dialect speech as well as the proponent's point of view. For only as research is read and analyzed does one become aware of further research needed. The following recommendations are made in terms of additional research needed.

1. There is need for an analysis of the child's perceptions of dialect speech as investigated by a white standard English speaking researcher.

2. The teacher's perception of Black dialect speech used in the classroom is worth of study.

3. Teachers need additional information about the most effective reading approaches for dialect speaking children as well as for all children.

4. There is need for a study which specifically investigates the dialect speaking child's ability to understand standard English directions given in the classroom. The Meuser study (1971) addressed this question incidentally with 160 kindergarten children in a southern city. A replication of this study with children in other urban areas should prove interesting.

5. Finally, a study is needed which tests the dialect speaking child's ability to learn to read from readers written in dialect speech compared with dialect speaking children learning to read from standard English material.

Answers to some, or all of these problems should provide further information to find the answer to why Black children show poor progress in reading.

Perhaps one reason why the subjects in this study are reading as well as they are is because they perceive the language they use in a positive way. Black children are so involved in their own language that it is extremely easy for them to verbalize in it and become almost too verbal for their teacher's comfort, if only allowed to do so. Moumouni (1968) said:

> The emotional importance of a language lies in the fact that it contains the voices of one's mother, father, brothers and sisters and one's dearest friends. Our deepest emotions and most intimate memories are tightly bound up with our native tongue (p. 108).

Black children will continue to use dialect speech for many years to come. The extent of the teacher's movement from standard English to Black dialect in terms of understanding, appreciation and acceptance, and the ability to understand how the child perceives his language might be the key to establishing a successful relationship with the Black child. Much of this relationship, to be at all successful, will be based on mutual respect, and feeling as good about the child as he feels about himself. This would seem to be a healthy, positive relationship on which to build a reading program. Many teachers are extremely sensitive to strengths of Black children and their language, leading to a positive teacher-child relationship. However, it really does not stop there, for in showing understanding and appreciation for the child and his dialect, one is really expressing the same for his culture and community.

BIBLIOGRAPHY

Bailey, B. L. "Concern for Special Curriculum Aspects: Bilingualism," Imperatives for Change: Proceedings of the New York State Education Department Conference on College and University Programs for Teachers of the Disadvantaged, ed. A. Jablonsky. New York: Yeshiva University, 1967.

Bailey, B. L. "Some Aspects of the Impact of Linguistics on Language Teaching in Disadvantaged Communities," Elementary English (May, 1968), 57-58.

Bailey, B. L. "Language and Communicative Styles of Afro-American Children in the United States." In A. Aarons, B. Gordon, W. Stewart (eds.), The Florida FL Reporter, Vol. 7, No. 1, Spring/Summer, 1969.

Baratz, J. C. "Teaching Reading in an Urban School System." In J. C. Baratz, and R. W. Shuy (eds.), Teaching Black Children to Read. Washington, D.C.: Center for Applied Linguistics, 1969.

Baratz, J. C. "Beginning Readers for Speakers of Divergent Dialects," Reading Goals for the Disadvantaged, International Reading Association, 1970a.

Baratz, J. C. "Relationship of Negro Non-Standard English Dialect Speech to Reading Achievement," unpublished paper, Education Study Center, 1970b.

Baratz, J. C. "Teaching Reading in an Urban Negro School System." In F. Williams (ed.), Language and Poverty. Chicago: Markham Publishing Co., 1971.

Baratz, J. C., and S. Baratz. "Early Childhood Intervantion: The Social Science Base of Institutional Racism," Harvard Educational Review, 40, No. 1 (Winter, 1970), 29-50.

Baratz, J. C., and R. W. Shuy (eds.), Teaching Black Children to Read. Washington, D.C.: Center for Applied Linguistics, 1969.

Cohen, A., and C. Cooper. "Seven Fallacies: RNading Retardation and the Urban Disadvantaged Beginning Reader." Reprinted from the Reading Teacher (October, 1972), 38-44.

Davis, F. B. Educational Measurements and Their Interpretation. Belmont, California: Wadsworth Publishing Co., 1965.

Deutsch, C. P. "Auditory Discrimination and Learning: Social Factors," Merrill-Palmer Quarterly, 10 (July, 1964), 277-296.

Dillard, J. L. Black English: Its History and Usage in the United
     States. New York: Random House, 1972.

Dolch, E. W. The Basic Sight Word Test on the Basic Sight Word
     Vocabulary. Champaign, Ill.: The Gerrard Press, 1942.

Du Bois, W. E. B. Souls of Black Folk. Chicago: A. C. McClurg
     Co., 1903.

Durrell, D., and H. Murphy. "The Auditory Discrimination Factor in
     Readiness and Reading Disability," Education, 73 (1953), 556-560.

Fleming, J. T. "Teachers Ratings of Urban Children's Reading Per-
     formance," Paper read at the American Educational Research
     Association Convention, 1970, Minneapolis, Minnesota.

Fryburg, E. L. "The Relations Among English Syntax, Methods of Instruc-
     tion and Reading Achievement of First Grade Disadvantaged Black
     Children." Unpublished Doctor's dissertation, New York University,
     1970.

Goodman, K. S. "Languages Children Bring to School and How to Build
     on it," Grade Teacher, 86 (March, 1969), 135-139.

Gottesman, R. L. "Auditory Discrimination Ability in Negro Dialect-
     Speaking Children," Journal of Learning Disorders, 5 (Fall, 1972),
     94-101.

Hensley, A., and E. Hatch. "Black High School Students' Reactions to
     Black Speakers of Standard and Black English." 1970 (mimeographed).

Ives, J. P., and S. Ives. "Contributions of Linguistics to Reading and
     Spelling." In National Society for the Study of Education.
     Linguistics in School Programs. LXIX Yearbook, Part II. Chicago:
     University of Chicago Press, 1970.

Johnson, K. R. "Teacher's Attitudes Toward the Nonstandard Negro
     Dialect--Let's Change it." Elementary English, 48 (February,
     1971), 176-184.

Johnson, K. R., and H. D. Simons. "Black Children and Reading," Phi
     Delta Kappa (January, 1972), 288-290.

Kaplan, R. "On a Note of Protest (in a Minor Key), Bidialectism vs.
     Bidialecticism," College English, 30 (February, 1969), 386-389.

Kligman, D. S., B. A. Cronnell, and G. B. Verna, "Black English Pro-
     nunciation and Spelling Performances," Elementary English, 49,
     No. 8 (December, 1972), 1247.

Labov, W. "States in the Acquisition of Standard English." In Roger
     W. Shuy (ed.), Social Dialects and Language Learning. Champaign,
     Ill.: National Council of Teachers of English, 1964, 77-103.

Labov, W. "Some Sources of Reading Problems for Negro Speakers of Non-Standard English." In New Directions in Elementary English. New York: National Council of Teachers of English, 1967a, 140-167.

Labov, W. "The Non-Standard VErnacular of the Negro Community: Some Practical Suggestions." Paper read at the Seminar in English and Language Arts, Temple University, May, 1967L.

Labov, W. "Some Sources of Reading Problems for Negro Speakers of Non-Standard English." In J. B. Baratz and R. W. Shuy (eds.), Teaching Black Children to Read. Washington, D.C.: Center for Applied Linguistics, 1969.

Labov, W. Language in the Inner City. Philadelphia: University of Pennsylvania Press, 1972.

Labov, W., P. Cohen, and C. Robbins. "A Preliminary Study of the Structure of English Used by Negro and Puerto Rican Speakers in New York City." New York: Columbia University, 1965. (Mimeographed.)

Leaverton, L., and M. R. Gladney. "A Model for Teaching Standard English to Non-Standard English Speakers," Elementary English, 45 (October, 1968), 758-763.

Lindeman, R. "Three Methods for Judging Contrasts Among K Means." New York: Teachers College, Columbia University, 1974. (Mimeographed.)

MacGinitie, W. "An Overview of Language Studies." Paper read at NDEA Institute for the Hearing Impaired, July, 1965, New York, p. 4.

Melmed, P. J. "Black English Phonology: The Question of Reading Interference." Unpublished Doctor's dissertation, University of California, 1970.

Moumouni, A. Education in Africa. New York: Frederick A. Praeger, 1968.

Mueser, A. M. "Effects of Different Reinforcers and Operant Level on Reading Task Behavior of Black Kindergarteners." Unpublished Doctor's dissertation, Yeshiva University, 1971, p. 77.

New York City Board of Education. "Approaches to Teaching Reading: Professional Seminars Unit" (Catherine Stern Approach, Initial Teaching Alphabet, Linguistic Approach, Basal Reader Program) 1967.

New York Times. "Decline Continues in Reading Ability of Pupils in City." November 19, 1972, p. 1.

New York Times. "Blacks in City Constitute Largest Group in School." October 23, 1973, p. 1.

New York Times. "Reading Scores in City on Rise." February 14, 1974, p. 1.

Nolan, P. S. "Reading Non-Standard Materials: A Study at Grades Two and Four," Child Development, 43 (1972), 1092-1097.

Putnam, G. N., and E. M. O'Hern. "The Status Significance of an Isolated Urban Dialect," Language, 31 (October -December, 1955), 1-32.

Rystrom, R., and A. Cowart. "Black Errors or White Teacher Biases?" Journal of Reading, 15 (January, 1972), 273-276.

Shuy, R. W. (ed.). Social Dialects and Language Learning. Champaign, Illinois: National Council of Teachers of English, 1964.

Singh, S., and J. W. Black. "Study of Twenty-Six Intervocalic Consonants as Spoken and Recognized by Four Language Groups," Journal of the Acoustical Society of America, 39 (1966), 372-387.

Smith, F. "Phonology and Orthography: Reading and Writing," Elementary English, 7 (1972), 1075.

Stewart, W. A. "Urban Negro Speech: Sociolinguistic Factors Affecting English Teaching." In R. W. Shuy (ed.), Social Dialects and Language Learning. Champaign, Illinois: National Council of Teachers of English, 1964.

Stewart, W. A. "On the Use of Negro Dialect in the Teaching of Reading." In J. C. Baratz and R. W. Shuy (eds.), Teaching Black Children to Read. 1969 excerpts reprinted in unpublished paper of J. C. Baratz, "A Review of Research on the Relationship of Black English to Reading," International Reading Association, Atlantic City (1971), 3.

Stewart, W. A. "Current Issues in the Use of Negro Dialect in Beginning Reading Texts," The Florida FL Reporter, 8, Nos. 1 and 2 (Spring/ Fall, 1970).

Stewart, W. A. "Continuity and Change in American Negro Dialects," Language and Poverty. Chicago, Illinois: Markham Press, 1971.

Thompson, B. "A Longitudinal Study of Auditory Discrimination," Journal of Educational Research, 56 (1963), 376-378.

Thorndike, R. (ed.). Educational Measurement, 2nd Ed. Washington, D.C.: American Council on Education, 1971.

Valentine, C. "Deficit, Difference, and Bicultural Models of Afro-American Behavior," Harvard Educational Review, 41, 2 (May, 1971), 10.

Venezky, R. L. "English Orthography: Its Graphical Structure and its Relation to Sound," Reading Research Quarterly, (1967), 75-105.

Venezky, R. L. "Linguistics and Spelling," N.S.S.E. Yearbook, Linguistics in School Programs. LXIX, Part II. Chicago: University of Chicago Press, 1970.

Wardhaugh, R. "Some Linguistic Insights into Reading Instruction." In A. C. Aarons, B. Gordon, and W. Stewart (eds.), Florida FL Reporter, 7, 1 (Spring/Summer, 1969), 110-111, 155-156.

Woodworth, W., and R. Salzer. "Black Children's Speech and Teacher's Evaluations," Urban Education, 6, 2/3 (July, 1971), 167.

APPENDIX A

Recording Sheet
Speech Characteristics

Instructions

PICTURES FOLDER

Put a (√) next to word when characteristic is present in child's speech

Add additional speech variations

TAPED STORY

Put a circle around word as child makes judgment

PHONICS SHEET

Put a check in proper box if child chose non-traditional orthography

Other phonological variables (switched)

peel   pail   picture
pitcher

substitution of medial "th" muvah favah	substitution of initial "th" dat day	r-lessness caa foh	l-lessness toos chirren	simplification of conso.clust's playin scrubbin cleanin	substitution of final "th" mouf teef baff	Use of "es" for plurals ghosses maskes
1. foh (M) four (G)	3. teeth (G) teef (M)	5. mouth (G) mouf (M)	7. baff (G) bath (M)	9. hepp (G) help (M)	11. pin (M) pen (G)	13. win (M) wind (G)
2. tesses (G) tests (M)	4. muvah (G) mother (M)	6. desses (M) desks (G)	8. liff (M) lift (G)	10. dey (M) they (G)	12. picture (M) pitcher (G)	14. blowin (M) blowing (G)

Name _____ Date _____ Grade _____ Age _____

PICTURE
FOLDER

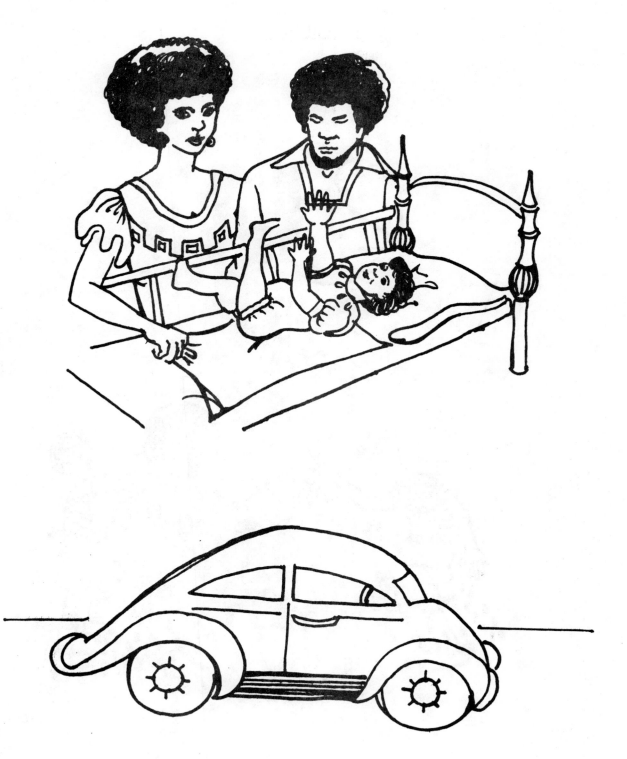

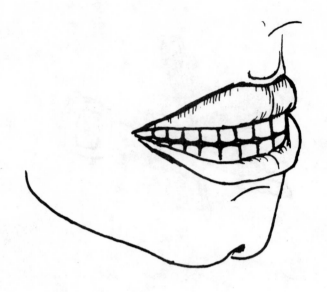

four	**4**	foh
caa		car
help		hepp
tools		toos

winn | wind

pen | pin

desses | desks

mother | muvah

pen		pin
blowin		blowing
children		chirren
mouth teef		mouf teeth